MW00987253

Cactus *of* TEXAS
FIELD GUIDE

by Nora and Rick Bowers
Stan Tekiela

Adventure Publications, Inc.
Cambridge, Minnesota

Our enduring gratitude to Matt Johnson, our good friend and cactus guru, for his patient tutoring over the years. Maybe one day it will stick. — **NORA and RICK**

To my wife, Katherine, and daughter, Abigail, with all my love. — **STAN**

Acknowledgments

A special thanks to Matt Johnson, who made this book possible by reviewing the range maps and the text, guiding us on field trips to Texas to photograph cacti and allowing us to photograph his Texas cactus plants in his beautiful backyard. We also thank Cathryn Hoyt and Marc Goff at the Chihuahuan Desert Nature Center in Fort Davis, Riverside Nature Center in Kerrville and Robbie Dudley at Judge Roy Bean Visitor Center in Langtry for allowing photography of their cacti. Our enduring gratitude to Bill Carr and Debbie Benish of The Nature Conservancy of Texas for making access possible to the beautiful and important Las Estrellas Preserve. We are also grateful to those responsible for the Flora of North America web site for making scientific information accessible to all.

Edited by Deborah Walsh

Contributing Editors: Brett Ortler and Sandy Livoti

Cover and book design by Jonathan Norberg

Cactus illustrations by Julie Martinez

Range maps produced by Anthony Hertzel, reviewed by Matt Johnson

Photo credits: Cover photo of Longmamma Pincushion by Rick and Nora Bowers. See pages 364-365 for photo credits by photographer and page number.

10 9 8 7 6 5 4 3 2 1

Table of Contents

TEXAS AND CACTI

Texas is a great place for anyone who loves plants—especially for those interested in cacti! From the hot arid deserts of far western Texas through the cooler central grasslands to the subtropical south, Texas is fortunate to have extremely diverse, often unique, and beautiful cacti. Texas is home to more species of cacti than any other state, including some rare miniature cacti found nowhere else in the United States.

Cactus of Texas Field Guide is designed to help the curious nature seeker easily identify 80 species in Texas. It is an all-photographic guide just for Texas, featuring full-color images of entire cacti, close-ups of cactus spines, vivid flowers, fruit and more. This is one in a series of unique field guides for Texas, including those for birds, mammals, trees and wildflowers.

WHAT IS A CACTUS?

Cacti are succulents—drought-tolerant plants that store large quantities of water in their fleshy (succulent) leaves, stems or roots. There are many families of succulent plants, differing mainly in the structure of their flowers. Cacti are members of one succulent family, the Cactaceae. So, although all cacti are succulents, not all succulents are cacti.

For the purposes of this book, a cactus is defined as having fleshy, leafless stems with waxy, water-retaining skin, and prickly spines emerging in clusters from specialized areas in the skin called areoles. Food production (photosynthesis) in cacti is mainly accomplished in the stems by enlarged green cells that also retain water. Spines provide shade for the stems, reducing water evaporation, and form a barrier that defends the plant from being eaten by animals. Cactus flowers are usually handsome, with many similar-looking petals and petal-like sepals, hundreds of pollen-bearing male flower parts (stamens) and a sticky female flower part (stigma). *Cactus of Texas Field Guide* will help you observe stems, spines, flowers and other basic characteristics so you can confidently identify different species.

IDENTIFICATION STEP-BY-STEP

In this field guide, cacti are organized by overall plant or stem shape. To aid identification, we've divided the cacti into general stem groups, and each of these groups has a color-coded thumb tab in the upper right-hand corner of the first description pages. We've described four different groups: small spineless cacti (blue tab), cacti with cylindrical stems (maroon tab), cacti with segmented stems (green tab) and cacti with angular stems (gold tab).

SMALL SPINELESS STEMS

CYLINDRICAL STEMS

SEGMENTED STEMS

ANGULAR STEMS

SUBGROUPS

A stem group may be broken down into subgroups. Each subgroup has a corresponding icon for easy identification; similar subgroups are placed together and have one icon. Each subgroup is loosely organized by stem size from small to large. This can be helpful when the plant you are trying to identify is at its mature height. The measurement given for each species is the typical height of the cactus as it is most commonly seen, with a few exceptions. Cacti vary throughout the year, shrinking during drought and cold and gaining height and girth during the warm rainy season.

The Small Spineless Stem Group

 This group contains only three small cacti that are spineless and have smooth or fissured skin. Often rare, these cacti have disk-shaped or dome-like stems with either shallow ribs or knobs (called tubercles) and hair-like wool in the areoles. They grow low to the ground (withdrawing to below ground level during drought) and are inconspicuous, which helps protect them from being eaten. Their flowers are large in proportion to their stems and sprout from the center of the tops of the stems. The small, fleshy fruit is dry when mature.

The Cylindrical Stem Group

If a cactus has cylindrical stems, it belongs in this group. The next step is to identify whether it is a pincushion, pineapple/beehive, fishhook, hedgehog or barrel cactus. Each of these five subgroups of cacti is represented by a unique icon in the thumb tabs.

 Pincushion cacti are short and round cacti that usually grow in clusters. Firm conical tubercles spiral around the stems. The tubercles are topped with a cluster of fine spines. Flowers appear in a ring at the top edges of the stems. Pincushion fruit lacks hair, scales or spines.

 Pineapple and beehive cacti appear so similar that they are combined into one subgroup with one thumb tab icon. Pineapple cacti are pineapple-shaped short plants, but vary in shape from somewhat globe-shaped to cylindrical. They usually have a single stem (sometimes small clusters) with tubercles arranged on vertical ribs rather than in spirals. Blossoms are short, stiff, funnel-shaped and appear in dense tufts at the tip of stems. Fruit is fleshy and scaly, drying when ripe in most species. Beehive cacti have globe-shaped stems with a flat top, much like a honeybee hive. Cone-shaped tubercles on the skin appear in spirals. Each tubercle has a groove on the upper side and a cluster of spines growing from the tip. Beehive cacti often grow as one stem, but some species appear in large cluster mounds. While similar to pincushion cacti, beehives differ because of the tubercle grooves, stouter spines, longer taproots and flowers that are densely clustered on top of the stems.

Fishhook cacti have upright stems of different shapes with well-defined rows of tubercles or prominent ribs that often twist around the stem. Some of these cacti remain unbranched with a single stem, while others form clumps of stems. Most of the cacti in the subgroup have tubercles that are grooved on their upper surfaces. These grooves contain nectar-producing glands and are packed with wool. All but one of these cacti have one or more hooked spines in each spine cluster. All have stout and formidable-looking spines, flowers that sprout from the tips of the stems and spineless fruit that either dries out when mature or remains only slightly fleshy.

Hedgehog cacti are taller and therefore appear slimmer than pincushions. Stems have vertical folds of ridges and grooves (called ribs) and often grow in clusters. Small to large flowers bloom just below the tips or along the sides of the stems, emerging through the skin above a mature spine cluster. The fruit of hedgehog cacti is spiny.

Barrel cacti are the largest of the cylindrical cacti, with thick, barrel-shaped stems as tall as 5 feet (1.5 m). Stem surfaces are ribbed and lined with stout spine clusters.

The Segmented Stem Group

Segmented cacti are shrubby, tree-like or low-growing mats. In this type of cactus, new stem segments, or joints, branch from the previous year's segments. Beginning as buds with tiny leaves, these grow and divide during the rainy season before growing spines. In addition to the usual spines, spine clusters have many tiny barbed bristles known as glochids. Prickly glochids are more easily felt than seen and present only in prickly pear, dog cholla and cholla cacti. There are three main subgroups of cacti with segmented stems, and each group is represented by its own thumb tab icon.

 Prickly pears have flat, paddle-shaped stems.

 Dog chollas have cylindrical stems and are low growing, creeping along the ground and forming dense mats.

 Chollas are upright tree- or shrub-like cacti, also with slender cylindrical stems.

Note: It is easy to identify cacti as prickly pears, but they are the most difficult cacti to categorize as a specific species. Even experts disagree on what characteristics should be used for species identification and, thus, how many species of prickly pears are found in Texas.

The Angular Stem Group

Two species of Texas cacti in the *Peniocereus* and *Acanthocereus* genera have angular stems that are triangular, square or 6-sided. These cacti have large white flowers that bloom during a single night.

 Desert Night-blooming Cereus is an inconspicuous, stick-like cactus with square or 6-sided stems.

 Barbed Wire Cactus has succulent triangular stems.

USING PHOTOS TO CONFIRM THE IDENTITY

After using the thumb tabs to narrow your choices, the last step is to confirm the identity of the cactus. First, compare it with the photos of entire plants and consider the information given about habitat and consult the range maps. Next, examine the spines and compare them with the inset photos. Since flowers or fruit can be a better indicator of a species, compare those photos as well. Use the rulers on page 368 to help estimate spine, flower and fruit sizes. Finally, look at the three photos above the Compare section to verify the identity of your cactus. These photos illustrate characteristics that differ among similar species. Or, if you think you know which cactus you're looking for, simply use the index.

SEASON OF BLOOM

Many cacti have a specific season of blooming. For example, you probably won't see the spring-blooming Heyder Pincushion flowering during summer or autumn. Knowing the season of bloom can help you narrow your selection as you try to identify a cactus. Since the weather in Texas ranges from the warmer subtropical climate in the southern part of the state to the colder areas in the hills of central Texas, we have identified the months in which a cactus normally blooms. Spring usually occurs from March through May, although some species, such as Davis Hedgehogs, bloom as early as February. Summer refers to June, July and August. Fall usually means September, October and November.

Some cacti do not bloom during a certain season, but flower anytime it rains in the warmer months. Interestingly, you must look for some cactus flowers at certain times of the day or night. For instance, Barbed Wire Cactus blooms from midnight to dawn, while Horse Crippler flowers open in midmorning and close at night.

HABITATS

Sometimes noting the habitat of a cactus in question can help determine its identity. Some cacti thrive only in specific habitats and at particular elevations. They may require certain types of soil, moisture, pH levels, fungi or nutrients. Other cacti are generalists and can grow in a wide variety of habitats. Noting the habitat surrounding a cactus is an important clue to its identity.

RANGE

The wide variety of habitats in Texas naturally restricts the range of many cacti that have specific habitat requirements. On the first description page for each cactus, a small range map indicates where in Texas you may find the cactus. Larger versions of these maps appear on pages 346-359. Description pages also contain text denoting the range for each cactus. Sometimes these maps and descriptions can help you eliminate a cactus from consideration based solely on its range. However, please keep in mind that the ranges indicate where the cactus is most commonly found. They are general guidelines only and there will certainly be exceptions.

COMPARE

Look-alike cacti can be difficult to tell apart. Three comparison photos at the top of description pages draw your attention to differing details of similar-looking species. To help you identify your cactus, the accompanying text contrasts these features and other attributes. Much of the detailed information in this section is unique and not found in other cactus field guides.

NOTES

The Notes are fun and fact-filled with many gee-whiz tidbits of interesting information such as historical uses, other common names, relationship of the species with insects, color variations and much more.

CAUTION

In the Notes, it is occasionally mentioned that parts of some cacti were used for medicine or food. While some find this interesting, DO NOT use this field guide to identify edible or medicinal plants. Please enjoy the cacti of Texas with your eyes or with your camera. In addition, please don't pick cactus flowers or fruit, cut stems or attempt to transplant any cacti. The flower of a plant is its reproductive structure, and if you pick a cactus flower you have limited its ability to reproduce. Transplanting cacti is another destructive occurrence. Most cacti need specific soil types, pH and moisture levels or temperatures to grow properly. If you attempt to transplant a cactus to a habitat that is not suitable for its particular needs, the plant most likely will die.

All cacti on public land in Texas are protected, and trespassing on private land is strictly prohibited. Some rare species, due to their dwindling populations, are protected by federal laws that forbid you to disturb the plants in any way. The good news is all of our Texas cacti are now available at local garden centers. These plants have been cultivated and have not been taken from the wild except by permit. Cacti are an important part of our natural environment, and leaving them healthy and unharmed will do a great deal to help keep the Lone Star State the exceptional place it is.

Enjoy the Wild Cacti!

Nora, Rick and Stan

CACTUS BASICS

It's easier to identify cacti and discuss them when you know the names of their different parts. For instance, it is more effective to use the word "glochids" to indicate hair-like spines than to try to describe them. The following illustrations point out the basic parts of various cacti. These are for informational purposes only and should not be confused with any specific cactus species.

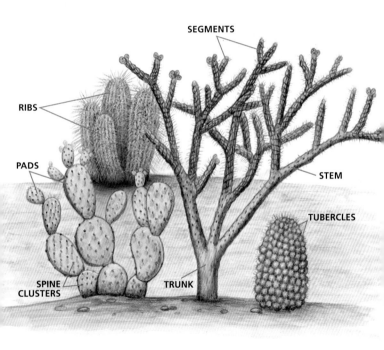

SEGMENTS

RIBS

PADS

STEM

TUBERCLES

SPINE
CLUSTERS

TRUNK

Spine Cluster

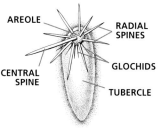

AREOLE
RADIAL SPINES
CENTRAL SPINE
GLOCHIDS
TUBERCLE

Flower

PETALS
STIGMA
ANTHERS
STYLE
SEPAL
FILAMENTS
OVARY

STIGMA + STYLE = **PISTIL**
ANTHERS + FILAMENTS = **STAMENS**

Stems

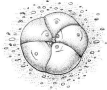

Small Spineless Stems
Living Rock Cactus, Peyote
and Star Cactus

Cylindrical Stems
pincushion,
pineapple/beehive, fishhook,
hedgehog and barrel

Segmented Stems
prickly pear, dog cholla
and cholla

Angular Stems
Desert Night-blooming Cereus,
Barbed Wire Cactus

spines

flower

fruit

Range Map

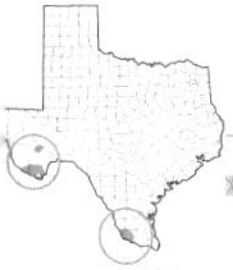

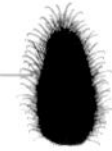

see page 346 for larger map

Stem Group Color Tab

CYLINDRICAL

Common Name

Scientific Name

Shape

Subgroup

Size: (H) average height of the mature cactus from ground to top; (W) average width of the mature cactus, for those occurring as a single stem

Shape: growth form and overall appearance, may include average width of a cluster of stems

Stem: number of stems and features such as color, stem segment size or protuberances (tubercles); may include other pertinent details

Spines: color and length

Spine Clusters: number of spines per cluster; brief description of central spines, radial spines and glochids

Flower: shape, color, position and size of flower or flower cluster

Blooming: month(s) when the flower blooms; may include related information

Fruit: overall description of pod such as shape, color, size, spines, tubercles, edibility, seeds or attachment

See pages 7-11 for more information about the stem group and subgroup designations.

Habitat: areas such as deserts, thorn scrub, grasslands or woodlands, along with elevation ranges; places where the cactus grows such as desert flats, canyons, valleys, clearings, plateaus, ridges, hilltops, slopes, mountains, outcrops, along washes; may include soil types

Range: part(s) of Texas where the cactus is found

 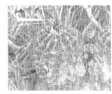 

Main species
description of features
shown in the image

Compare species (page)
contrasting description of
features

Compare species (page)
contrasting description of
other features

Compare: Notes about other species that look similar and the pages on which they can be found. Up-close color photos show differences among stems, spines, tubercles, flowers, fruit or other key characteristics.

Notes: Helpful identification information such as remarkable features, history, name origins and other interesting gee-whiz nature facts.

tubercle

Living Rock Cactus
Ariocarpus fissuratus

see page 346 for
larger map

Size: H ground level to ¾" (2 cm); W 2-5" (5-13 cm); often below ground level in drought

Shape: flat disk-like stem with a dimpled center; resembles a multiple-pointed star

Stem: single greenish gray or orangish brown stem with overlapping rings of grooved triangular bumps (tubercles); each leathery flattened tubercle, 1" (2.5 cm) wide, is topped with a woolly triangular area (areole); the center of the stem top has grayish white wool

Spines: spineless

Spine Clusters: widely spaced areoles with short gray wool

Flower: group of wide pink blossoms at the center of stem top; each flower, 1-2" (2.5-5 cm) wide, has outer paler petals with darker pink midstripes around orangish yellow male flower parts (stamens) and a white female flower part (stigma)

Blooming: September-November

Fruit: smooth, thin, cylindrical or pear-shaped pod, ½-1" (1-2.5 cm) long, greenish white when ripe, slightly fleshy but soon drying to brown with shiny black seeds; remains firmly attached in the woolly center, maturing in June-July the following year

Habitat: desert scrub between 1,500-4,500' (460-1,370 m); flats, hills, with lechuguillas and other shrubs; limestone rocky soils

Range: far western Texas and an area east of the Pecos River along the Rio Grande

Living Rock Cactus
rough grooved
triangular tubercles

Star Cactus *(pg. 31)*
smooth ribs dotted
with white

Star Cactus *(pg. 31)*
pale yellow, not
pink, flowers

Compare: The also spineless, rare Star Cactus (pg. 31), might at first be mistaken for Living Rock Cactus. However, Living Rock has very wrinkled, grooved, triangular tubercles that are quite different from the white-dotted smooth ribs of Star. Also, Star has pale yellow, rather than pink flowers. Confusingly, Living Rock sometimes is called Star Cactus, sharing the common name.

Notes: Living Rock Cactus is a spineless, flat-topped, greenish gray disk forming a multiple-pointed, leathery star. Grows just above or below the ground. Found in stony ground and often mistaken for one of the rocks. Withdrawing below ground level during drought protects this tough little plant from moisture loss and being trampled by careless feet. Thus it is difficult to see until, surprisingly, a showy clump of pink flowers appears in the fall. The genus name *Ariocarpus*, derived from both Latin and Greek words, means "pear-shaped fruit." The small fruit, hidden in the wool at the center of the stem, ripens about 8-9 months later.

Of six species in the genus, all of which occur in northeastern Mexico, this is the only one found in the United States. Slow growing, it takes as long as a decade to reach maturity and bloom–a wild plant can take 80 years to reach a width of 4 inches (10 cm). Revered by the Tarahumara, Huichol and Kickapoo Indians of Mexico, who used stem pieces to treat fever, tuberculosis and wounds. Containing hallucinogens, the stems were also ingested as a part of spiritual ceremonies.

woolly areoles

flower

Spineless

Peyote
Lophophora williamsii

see page 346 for larger map

Size: H ¾-2" (2-5 cm)

Shape: clumps of dome-shaped or flat disk-shaped stems (usually branching into less than 12, but up to as many as 50) or a single stem; stems have a deeply dimpled center

Stem: smooth, soft, grayish or bluish green stems, each 2-5" (5-13 cm) wide, with 5-13 (usually 8) broad ribs separated by shallow grooves; ribs are lined with 6-sided bumps (tubercles); each tubercle, 1" (2.5 cm) wide, is tipped with a woolly circular area (areole); woolly and grayish white stem top

Spines: spineless

Spine Clusters: widely spaced areoles with short gray wool

Flower: few pale or rose pink blossoms at centers of stem tops; each flower, ⅝-1" (1.5-2.5 cm) wide, has inner petals with darker midstripes around yellow and white or magenta male flower parts (stamens) and a white female flower part (stigma)

Blooming: March-May, sometimes June-September

Fruit: smooth, thin, cylindrical or club-shaped pod, ½-1" (1-2.5 cm) long, pink and slightly fleshy, but soon drying to translucent brownish white; containing black seeds; abruptly elongating and emerging above stem wool nearly 1 year after blooming

Habitat: desert scrub and thorn scrub between 150-6,000' (50-1,830 m); flats, hills, under shrubs, in rock crevices; limestone soils

Range: Big Bend area of far western Texas, along the Rio Grande and the far southern portion of the state

Peyote
smooth 6-sided
tubercles make the
ribs lumpy

Living Rock Cactus
(pg. 23)
wrinkled and grooved
triangular tubercles

Star Cactus *(pg. 31)*
smooth, not lumpy, ribs
dotted with white

Compare: The also spineless Living Rock Cactus (pg. 23) might be mistaken for a partially buried Peyote stem. However, Living Rock has very wrinkled and grooved tubercles, quite unlike the smooth, 6-sided tubercles of Peyote. The rare Star Cactus (pg. 31) is more similar to Peyote. Star's spineless smooth ribs dotted heavily with white can easily be distinguished from Peyote's lumpy ribs, which lack white dots.

Notes: Known for its very slow growth, taking decades to mature and bloom. This bluish gray miniature cactus has dome-shaped stems that grow above the ground or partially buried, with only the flat disk-shaped tops showing. Often branches into as many as 50 smooth spineless stems, but can grow as a solitary stem. Peyote is widespread in Chihuahuan Desert scrub and Tamaulipan thorn scrub in southwestern Texas, and throughout northeastern Mexico.

Famous for its psychoactive alkaloids (primarily mescaline), Peyote has a more than 6,000-year history of ritual religious and medicinal use by American Indians. Common name is from *peyotl*, the ancient Aztec word for this sacred cactus. Also called Divine Cactus. Federal law prohibits non-Indians from possessing Peyote, but allows its collection by American Indians for use in their religious ceremonies. Illegal collection by others for its hallucinogenic properties, as well as the severe loss of its habitat (especially thorn scrub in southern Texas), has greatly diminished the wild populations of Peyote in the United States.

woolly areoles

flower

fruit

SMALL SPINELESS

Spineless

Star Cactus
Astrophytum asterias

see page 346 for
larger map

Size: H 1-2½" (2.5-6 cm); W 2-6" (5-15 cm)

Shape: flattened round stem with pie-shaped ribs

Stem: single smooth, hard, orangish-to-brownish green stem with 8 broad pie-shaped ribs separated by grooves; each rib has a shallow ridge lined with a few larger round areas (areoles) filled with yellow or gray wool; each groove lined with many round dots of bright white wool

Spines: spineless

Spine Clusters: widely spaced areoles with short gray wool

Flower: several pale yellow blossoms at the center of stem top; each flower, 1½-2" (4-5 cm) wide, has long fringed petals with red bases around red and yellow flower parts

Blooming: March-May, sometimes after summer rains

Fruit: fuzzy oval pod, ⅝-¾" (1.5-2 cm) long, green or pink, covered with yellowish brown wool; drying and splitting open when mature, containing shiny dark brown seeds; produces fruit April-June and in autumn following summer flowering

Habitat: thorn scrub between 65-325' (20-100 m); gravelly hills, among grasses, beneath shrubs; sometimes in clay soils in bottomlands between hills; rarely, unprotected in the open

Range: limited to one county in southern Texas

Star Cactus
starfish-like outline
on stem

Living Rock Cactus
(pg. 23)
multiple-pointed
star shape

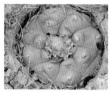

Peyote *(pg. 27)*
1-2 woolly areoles per rib

Compare: From above, the grooves between the ribs of a partially buried Star Cactus look like an outline of an eight-pointed starfish. Living Rock Cactus (pg. 23) stem is star-shaped with many more points. Young stems of Peyote (pg. 27), before they develop the lumpy ribs of mature plants, look like the spineless smooth ribs of Star. However, Star's ribs are dotted with a line of gray woolly round areas (areoles), while Peyote has only 1-2 areoles on each of the eight sections of the stem.

Notes: Genus name *Astrophytum* comes from the Greek words for "star plant" and refers to the star outline created by the stem grooves. Also called Sand Dollar Cactus for the marine animal this cactus more closely resembles. Grows mostly buried, with only the top of stem showing just above or below ground level. Often covered with grass or the leaves of the shrubs under which it grows. Thus, it is difficult to spot even knowing the plant is somewhere present.

One of four species in the genus, Star Cactus is the only one that occurs in the United States. A very rare cactus found in only two populations–in Starr County, Texas and Tamaulipas, Mexico–with only about 2,000 plants still in the wild. Overcollecting by cactus enthusiasts and loss of habitat have contributed to its endangered status. The survival of this cactus in one of the last areas of undisturbed thorn scrub in southern Texas is possibly almost entirely due to protection given it by The Nature Conservancy. Plants propagated by seed are available from accredited plant nurseries.

spines

fruit

CYLINDRICAL

Pincushion

Golf Ball Pincushion
Mammillaria lasiacantha

see page 346 for larger map

Size: H ¹/₂-1³/₈" (1-3.5 cm); W ³/₄-1¹/₂" (2-4 cm)

Shape: tiny, flat-topped, round or short cylindrical cactus

Stem: single stem with closely spaced conical bumps (tubercles); each tubercle topped with and obscured by a dense cluster of spines; outer portion of the stem contains a milky or clear sap

Spines: white or pinkish white, tipped with pinkish brown; less than ¹/₅" (.5 cm) long

Spine Clusters: densely overlapping clusters; each cluster has woolly white fuzz and 40-60 (can have up to 90) tiny, bristle-like radial spines radiating outward in layers from the center of cluster and curving inward against the stem; lacks central spines

Flower: cup-shaped, white-to-pale pink flowers forming a ring near the center of top of stem; each bloom, ¹/₃-¹/₂" (.8-1 cm) wide, has darker pink or brown midstripes on slender petals surrounding cream-colored flower parts

Blooming: February-March; flowers bloom for 2-3 days, closing at night

Fruit: smooth club-shaped pod, ¹/₂-³/₄" (1-2 cm) long, turns scarlet red, contains tiny black seeds; ripens June-August

immature plant

Habitat: desert scrub and mountains between 1,500-4,500' (460-1,370 m); flats, rocky hills, limestone or volcanic gravel slopes, among lechuguillas

Range: far western Texas

Golf Ball Pincushion
layers of spines obscure
green stem

Button Cactus *(pg. 43)*
single layer of spines per
cluster allows green stem
color to show

Button Cactus *(pg. 43)*
slim fruit packed into tight
cluster atop stem

Compare: Very similar in appearance to the tiny Button Cactus (pg. 43), which is not closely related. Button has a single layer of radial spines that does not always obscure the green color of the stem. Button's fruit are packed in a tight cluster at the very center of the top of the stem, rather than forming a small ring near the center like Golf Ball Pincushion fruit.

Notes: Named for the size and shape of the mature plant, this miniature, grayish white cactus is usually partially buried, with only the top ½ inch (1 cm) of its stem protruding above the ground. The plants can grow to a height of 3 inches (7.5 cm) and nearly as wide, but are usually less than half that tall. Immature plants are smaller than the diameter of a quarter.

Golf Ball Pincushion has the widest distribution of any small cacti in far western Texas and is one of the first to bloom in early spring. White-to-pale pink flowers form a small ring atop the cactus. Other species of tiny cacti are frequently found growing near it on the bare rocky limestone hills that these small plants favor.

Species name *lasiacantha* means "woolly spine" in Greek and refers to the interlacing layers of numerous white spines covering the entire stem. With no central spines and the points of the radial spines pressed tightly into the stem, it can be handled without being pricked. Sometimes called Lace-spine Pincushion. Found from New Mexico east through Texas and south into Mexico.

spines

flower

fruit

see page 347 for
larger map

CYLINDRICAL

Pincushion

Ping Pong Ball Cactus
Epithelantha bokei

Size: H ¾-1¼" (2-3 cm); W ¾-2" (2-5 cm)

Shape: disk-shaped or short cylindrical stem, flat or dimpled on top; sometimes branching into a cluster of a few stems

Stem: single or multiple smooth stems; each shiny stem appears white, clothed in a covering of highly reflective, densely woven spines that totally hide the green stem color and the very small bumps (tubercles); sometimes the top of stem has a swirl of fine long white hairs

Spines: white or yellowish white, less than ³⁄₁₀" (.7 cm) long

Spine Clusters: densely packed, partially overlapping clusters; each tiny cluster has many layers of 33-40 miniscule hair-like spines pressed tightly against the stem

Flower: tuft of partially translucent, silvery white or pale pink blossoms at center of stem tops and protruding above the spines; each funnel-shaped flower, ½-⅔" (1-1.6 cm) wide, has outer petals with green midstripes, pink or cream-colored male flower parts (stamens) and a white female flower part (stigma)

Blooming: May-June; opening midafternoon, closing at night, lasting 2-3 days

Fruit: smooth cylindrical red pod, ½" (1 cm) long, fleshy, containing glossy black seeds

dehydrated stem
collapsed to ground

Habitat: deserts between 2,300-4,400' (700-1,340 m); barren rocky limestone ridges, hills

Range: restricted to the Big Bend area in far western Texas

Ping Pong Ball Cactus
shorter, finer spines;
appears smooth and white

Button Cactus (pg. 43)
slightly fuzzier appearance

Golf Ball Pincushion
(pg. 35)
fuzzier with rounded top

Compare: Most similar to Button Cactus (pg. 43), which occurs in the same areas. The fuzzier Button differs by having slightly longer, but still tiny, spines that do not fully obscure the green stem color. Ping Pong Ball Cactus has shorter, finer spines that give it the appearance of being clothed in smooth woven white cloth. The fuzzier Golf Ball Pincushion (pg. 35) also looks like Ping Pong Ball, which is flatter on top.

Notes: A small, low-growing cactus so densely covered with layers of reflective, hair-like spines that the plant appears completely white. Spines protect many cacti from being eaten, but for cacti from intensely hot, sunny deserts, a complete covering of spines is more important for providing shade. Such is the case in Ping Pong Ball Cactus–the spines heavily shade the stem, but are so soft they don't deter an animal from eating the cactus. Usually partly buried, with only about 1 inch (2.5 cm) of the stem showing above the ground. In drought, the stem collapses in folds to ground level to conserve moisture. Heat tolerant up to 140°F (60°C).

Large compared to the plant, the delicate silvery white flowers appear atop the stem, protruding well above the spines. Threatened by collecting and development, this beautiful little cactus is in the Center for Plant Conservation's National Collection of Endangered Plants. Found in only 16 sites in Texas and nowhere else in the United States. The species name is for Norman H. Boke, who was the first to thoroughly investigate this cactus.

spines

fruit

CYLINDRICAL

Pincushion

Button Cactus
Epithelantha micromeris

see page 347 for
larger map

Size: H ½-2" (1-5 cm); W ¾-1½" (2-4 cm)

Shape: round or egg-shaped stem, flat or slightly rounded on top; sometimes branching into small clumps

Stem: single or multiple fuzzy stems; stem appears ashy gray and has numerous shallow bumps (tubercles) arranged in tight spirals around the stem; tubercles and green stem color mostly obscured by spines; stem top is woolly with a swirl of fine long white hairs

Spines: whitish gray, less than ³⁄₁₀" (.7 cm) long

Spine Clusters: tiny clusters that do not overlap; each cluster has an orange center and 1-3 layers of 20-35 tiny spines pressed tightly against the stem

Flower: tuft of partly translucent, pale pink or yellow blooms at center of stem top, with tips barely protruding above the spines; each small flower, less than ⅕" (.5 cm) wide, has fringed outer petals, pink or creamy yellow male flower parts (stamens) and a white female flower part (stigma)

Blooming: February-April; opening in morning, closing by midafternoon, lasting 1-2 days

Fruit: smooth thin cylindrical pod, ½-¾" (1-2 cm) long, red fruit wall slightly fleshy but soon dries and becomes papery thin; lacks pulp; contains glossy black seeds; ripens April-June

Habitat: deserts and grasslands from 1,300-5,000' (395-1,525 m); barren rocky limestone and volcanic ridges and hills

Range: Big Bend area of far western Texas, plus small areas extending east of the Pecos River and into the west central portion of the state

Button Cactus
slightly coarser spine clusters do not overlap, allowing green stem to show

Ping Pong Ball Cactus
(pg. 39)
stem folds allow stem to slump down in drought

Ping Pong Ball Cactus
(pg. 39)
flower larger and protrudes above spines

Compare: The very similar and closely related Ping Pong Ball Cactus (pg. 39) has stem folds called slump rings, formed when the stem collapses downward in drought; the fuzzier Button Cactus does not show these rings. Ping Pong Ball also has larger flowers that protrude above the spines at the top of stem, whereas only the tips of Button flowers show above the spines.

Notes: This miniature cactus appears ashy gray and grows as a single, rough-textured stem or (less often) branches into small clumps. Grows above ground, not partially buried. The genus name is derived from the Greek words for "flower at the top of the nipple," referring to the blooms arising from the top of the bumps (tubercles), not from between the tubercles as they do in the *Mammillaria* genus. Button Cacti the size of a penny are mature enough to flower. The flowers of this species are among the smallest of cactus flowers and are self-fertilizing. Up to a dozen slender fruit result, forming a clump on top of the stem, drying and becoming papery thin. Fruit and flowers can be on the plant simultaneously.

Cacti in the genus *Epithelantha* contain hallucinogens. Tarahumara Indians of northern Mexico ingest Button Cactus to stimulate and protect runners. They also consume it in rituals, believing it enables the user to perceive witches. More widespread than Ping Pong Ball, Button also occurs in Arizona and New Mexico, and in Chihuahua, Mexico.

spines

flower

fruit

see page 347 for larger map

CYLINDRICAL

Pincushion

Texas Pincushion
Mammillaria prolifera

Size: H ½-2" (1-5 cm)

Shape: dense mounds, 12" (30 cm) wide, with 12-20 round or egg-shaped stems of varying heights

Stem: multiple fuzzy stems, each ½-2" (1-5 cm) wide, with closely spaced cylindrical bumps (tubercles); each tubercle topped with and mostly hidden by a tangled cluster of spines; woolly white hairs between some of the tubercles

Spines: translucent and white or pale yellow; each central spine has a tan base and an outer half of reddish brown or black; less than ½" (1 cm) long

Spine Clusters: densely overlapping clusters; each circular area (areole) has woolly white fuzz, 8-11 central spines pointing outward in all directions or pressed against the stem, and 30-60 flexible or soft, hair-like, pale radial spines that curl outward in layers from the center of cluster

Flower: funnel-shaped, pale yellow or apricot flowers forming a ring near the center of tops of stems; each bloom, ½" (1 cm) wide, has darker midstripes on slender pointed petals surrounding cream and yellow flower parts

Blooming: March

Fruit: smooth, club-shaped or oval pod, ¾" (2 cm) long, turning pink or red, juicy, containing tiny black seeds; ripens 2-3 months after blooming

Habitat: bases of limestone cliffs up to 1,500' (460 m); rocky ridges, ledges, among shrubs and grasses, in deep soils

Range: west central and southern Texas

Texas Pincushion
curling, tangled layers of
soft radial spines

Rattail Pincushion *(pg. 63)*
dense white radial spines
make stems look similar to
Texas Pincushion

Rattail Pincushion *(pg. 63)*
radial spines are straight
and inflexible

Compare: Rattail Pincushion (pg. 63), with its dense layers of white radial spines and protruding brown central spines, can look very similar to Texas Pincushion. A closer inspection of the radial spines shows the difference–Texas has soft, curling, hair-like radial spines, whereas Rattail spines are straight and stiff.

Notes: Texas Pincushion is a small fuzzy cactus that branches when young, often into dense clumps of stems of varying heights. Sometimes the stems are packed so closely together that the mound looks like one larger stem. Easily identified at all ages by its curly, hair-like, white radial spines. Also known as Hair-covered Cactus. Growing under shrubs or grasses, this little plant is often overlooked since it can be covered up by other vegetation.

Found only in Texas in the United States, but also occurs in the wild in Mexico and West Indies. Commonly cultivated, as it is an easy plant to grow indoors on a window sill. The flowers are self-fertilized and produce bright red fruit. Both the flowers and fruit are present on the plant at the same time, with fruit from the previous year remaining on the plant through blooming time the next year. In the mid-1700s, Texas Pincushion was the second species in the *Mammillaria* genus to be discovered.

spines

flower

fruit

Heyder Pincushion
Mammillaria heyderi

see page 347 for larger map

Size: H ¾-2" (2-5 cm); W 3-6" (7.5-15 cm)

Shape: low-growing, disk-shaped cactus with a flat top

Stem: single stem covered with conical green bumps (tubercles), each topped with a cluster of spines; stem has a milky white sap

Spines: grayish white or reddish brown with dark tips; ¼-½" (.6-1.1 cm) long

Spine Clusters: each cluster has 1 short, rigid, outward-pointing central spine within a circle of 13-17 needle-like radial spines hugging the stem; lowest radials are longest and stoutest

Flower: small cream or light pink blossoms in a ring at the top of stem; each flower, 1-1½" (2.5-4 cm) wide, has a wide brownish green or pink stripe on the petals and a pink and green center

Blooming: February-April

Fruit: conical green pod, ½-1⅜" (1-3.5 cm) long, with fleshy walls and tiny reddish brown seeds; ripens 6 months to a year after blooming, elongating into a cylindrical, bright red pod

Habitat: desert scrub, grasslands and thorn scrub up to 4,600' (1,400 m); rocky limestone hills, washes, among grasses or under shrubs

Range: far western, southern and south central Texas; also a portion of the northwestern part of the state

  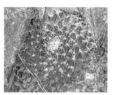

Heyder Pincushion
13-17 needle-like
radial spines

Little Pincushion *(pg. 55)*
5-7 stouter radial spines

Little Pincushion *(pg. 55)*
looks similar to Heyder

Compare: Heyder looks much like Little Pincushion (pg. 55), but they can be distinguished from each other by their radial spines. Little has 5-7 relatively stout radial spines, whereas Heyder has 13-17 needle-like radial spines.

Notes: A low, flat or round cactus with a stem that contracts in winter to just above ground level or sometimes below. Grows among grasses or hides under shrubs and is often overlooked until it blooms. Flowers open at midday, close at night and last for 3-4 days. Some cactus lovers searching for a glimpse of this interesting plant have nearly walked on it while trying to find it. Ripe fruit, often present with the pale flowers, is the product of blooms from the previous year.

Both Heyder and Little Pincushions are also called Cream Pincushion, being the only Texas cacti that have a milky sap. Pincushions with this latex are sold in the drug stalls of Mexico and used as folk remedies. Tarahumara Indians of Mexico used this sap for headaches, ear problems and more.

Found in Texas, southeastern Arizona, southern New Mexico, southwestern Oklahoma and northeastern Mexico. Cold hardy and frequently cultivated, this is one of the easiest (and slowest) pincushion cacti to grow.

spines

flower

fruit

Pincushion

Little Pincushion
Mammillaria meiacantha

see page 347 for larger map

Size: H 1-2" (2.5-5 cm); W 2¾-6½" (7-16 cm)

Shape: low-growing, disk-shaped cactus with a depressed or flat top

Stem: single stem covered with closely spaced and prominent conical green bumps (tubercles), each topped with a cluster of spines; stem produces a milky white sap

Spines: pinkish or yellowish brown to gray with dark tips; ⅕-⅝" (.5-1.5 cm) long

Spine Clusters: 6-10 straight spines per cluster; each cluster has 1 central spine projecting upward from the top rim of a circle of 5-7 stout radial spines that point outward; sometimes lacks a central spine

Flower: cup-shaped, white-to-pale pink flowers form a ring at the top of stem; each bloom, ¾-1¼" (2-3 cm) wide, has pink or lavender midstripes on slender petals surrounding cream-colored male flower parts (anthers) and a pale green female flower part (stigma)

Blooming: March-May, sometimes into June

Fruit: broadly club-shaped green pod, ¾-1¼" (2-3 cm) long, turns pink or dull red, contains tiny reddish brown seeds; ripens several months after flowering

CYLINDRICAL

Habitat: desert scrub, grasslands and oak/pine/juniper woodlands between 3,000-7,300' (915-2,225 m); rocky hills and ridges, among grasses, beneath oaks

Range: far western Texas

Little Pincushion
central spine points
upward, radial spines
point outward

Heyder Pincushion
(pg. 51)
central spine points out,
radials spread nearly flat

Heyder Pincushion
(pg. 51)
bright red fruit

Compare: The closely related Heyder Pincushion (pg. 51) overlaps in range and looks very much like Little Pincushion, but Heyder has one dark-tipped central spine in each cluster pointing directly outward. In contrast, Little has one central spine that points upward and looks much like its radial spines. Little has pink or dull red fruit, while Heyder has fruit that is bright red when ripe.

Notes: Also called Cream Pincushion for its milky sap, this broad flat cactus usually is less than 6½ inches (16 cm) wide, but can grow to a width of 12 inches (30 cm). It is the widest of any pincushion in Texas, but is often covered with grasses and not easily spotted, especially in drought, when the stem contracts to below ground level. Following rain, the stem expands upward, becoming more noticeable. If growing in shade, also becomes somewhat taller and rounded on top, reaching a height of 3-4 inches (7.5-10 cm).

Blooms open in March to May, forming a wreath atop the cactus. Pink or dull red fruit develops and ripens in 2-3 months, but is seldom seen since birds and small mammals love to eat it.

Tolerant of wide variations in temperature, this cactus is abundant in the mountains west of the Pecos River and in deserts near the Rio Grande in Big Bend National Park. Species name *meiacantha* means "fewer spines" in Greek, comparing Little Pincushion's smaller number of spines with other pincushion cacti.

spines

flower

Longmamma Pincushion
Mammillaria sphaerica

see page 347 for larger map

Size: H 1½-2" (4-5 cm)

Shape: lumpy mounds, up to 12" (30 cm) wide, of 10-30 many-branched stems

Stem: multiple knobby, rounded, pale green stems, each 2-3" (5-7.5 cm) wide, with large prominent conical bumps (tubercles) spreading outward; each tubercle is soft and tipped with sparse thin spines

Spines: yellowish white, less than ⅔" (1.6 cm) long

Spine Clusters: barely overlapping, sparse clusters; each cluster has 1 rigid, outward-pointing, straight central spine and 12-14 bristle-like gray radial spines

Flower: large, fragrant, lemon yellow flowers atop stems; each bloom, 2-3" (5-7.5 cm) wide, has wedge-shaped pointed petals; center has orangish yellow male flower parts (stamens) swirled around a pale yellow female flower part (stigma)

Blooming: July-August

Fruit: smooth, oval, dark green pod, ½" (1 cm) long, juicy throughout, containing brown seeds; does not ripen for many months after blooming (May of the following year), when it turns greenish white or dull pinkish tan; ripe fruit has a sweet aroma and an apple-like flavor

Habitat: thorn scrub up to 1,000' (305 m); plains, slopes, in the shade under other plants; gravelly soils

Range: southern Texas

Longmamma Pincushion
long conical tubercles with
sparse fine spines

**Big-needle Beehive
Cactus** *(pg. 139)*
mounds have very large,
conspicuous tubercles

**Big-needle Beehive
Cactus** *(pg. 139)*
stouter spines and lengthwise tubercle groove

Compare: Where overlapping in range in southern Texas, mounds
of Big-needle Beehive Cactus (pg. 139) with its many stems and
unusually large protuberances (tubercles) can look very similar
to Longmamma Pincushion. A closer inspection will show the
differences–Longmamma has sparse thin spines, while Big-needle
Beehive has stouter spines and the tubercle groove typical of beehive cacti. When blooming, a glance is sufficient to distinguish
between the two, since Big-needle has pink, not yellow, flowers.

Notes: The genus *Mammillaria* is named for the shape of the
tubercles. Also called Longmamma Nipple Cactus, both common
names of this plant come from its unusually large, conical tubercles
that cause the mound of stems to appear lumpy.

The sparse fine spines don't cover up the unusual, pale green stem
color at all, but when the large yellow blooms appear, the stems are
barely visible. Fragrant flowers open in the day, thus are probably
pollinated by native wild bees and other insects. The resulting green
fruit look like deformed, oversized tubercles until ripening to
greenish white, dull tan or maroon nearly nine months later.

Although often pictured as associated with deserts, cacti are actually
most diverse and abundant in dry parts of the tropics such as thorn
scrub of subtropical southern Texas. Fairly common in the state,
Longmamma also grows in dense colonies in the dry tropical forest
on the Gulf Coast in Mexico.

spines

flower

fruit

Rattail Pincushion
Mammillaria pottsii

see page 348 for
larger map

Size: H 2½-6" (6-15 cm)

Shape: small clumps of slim cylindrical stems branching from the base; can be a single stem

Stem: upright rigid stems, each ¾-1⅜" (2-3.5 cm) wide, wrapped with spirals of bumps (tubercles); numerous short spines totally cover tubercles and the bluish green stem color; white wool found in spaces between tubercles is longer on the top of stem

Spines: mostly white, gray or tan; often tipped with reddish brown or bluish gray; ¼-⅝" (.6-1.5 cm) long

Spine Clusters: densely overlapping clusters; each cluster has 6-12 stout dark-tipped central spines pointing outward and 37-49 bristle-like white radial spines pressed flat against the stem; 1 main central spine (pointing outward and curving upward) is bluish gray or reddish brown

Flower: small blooms, rusty or deep red, form a ring near the tops of stems; each vase-shaped flower, ½" (1 cm) wide, opens only partially and has a single layer of pale-edged petals curling backward at their tips; center made up of pale yellow male flower parts (anthers) and a pink female flower part (stigma)

Blooming: February-March; opening in late morning, closing at night, lasting 3-6 days

Fruit: smooth club-shaped red pod, ½-¾" (1-2 cm) long, has fleshy walls; edible, contains small brown seeds

Habitat: desert scrub from 2,800-4,000' (855-1,220 m); rocky slopes, gravelly flats, mesas, among creosote bushes or lechuguillas; volcanic or limestone soils

Range: Big Bend area of far western Texas

Rattail Pincushion
flowers located ¾ inch
(2 cm) below stem tip

Sneed Beehive Cactus
(pg. 143)
stems look a lot like Rattail

Sneed Beehive Cactus
(pg. 143)
flowers at very tip of stem

Compare: Rattail Pincushion looks much like the most common variety of Sneed Beehive Cactus (pg. 143), which also has small cylindrical stems covered by dense white spines. Like most beehive cacti, Sneed Beehive flowers clump right at the tip of the stem, and when in bloom, this feature most easily distinguishes it from Rattail. Rattail flowers form a ring just below the stem tip.

Notes: Rattail Pincushion forms small clumps of slender cylindrical stems covered with a dense mesh of white spines, with the longest dark central spine in each spine cluster protruding and curving upward. Thus, each stem resembles a tall pincushion stuck with pins. Blooms in very early spring, with unremarkable small flowers that appear to never fully open. The flowers are pollinated by small native bees, with the resulting fruit ripening in April.

The genus *Mammillaria* includes plants commonly called pincushion or nipple cacti and is one of the most diverse of cactus genera, with about 164 species. The greatest number of pincushion cacti occurs in Mexico, but they also are found in West Indies and Central America. Comparatively, Texas has very few–only seven species of pincushion cacti grow in the state. Rattail Pincushion just crosses the border from Mexico into the southern Big Bend area in the United States. Specifically, this cactus is easily seen on rocky limestone slopes on the north side of Highway 170, west of Terlingua, Texas.

spines

fruit

CYLINDRICAL

Pincushion

Arizona Fishhook Pincushion
Mammillaria grahamii

see page 348 for
larger map

Size: H 3-6½" (7.5-16 cm)

Shape: dense clumps of 1-9 (can have as many as 30) cylindrical or round stems

Stem: multiple stiff stems, each 1½-2¾" (4-7 cm) wide, covered with conical bumps (tubercles) that wind around the stem in spirals, but which are partially hidden by the spine clusters

Spines: mostly white or gray, ¼-1" (.6-2.5 cm) long

Spine Clusters: overlapping clusters; each cluster has 1-3 reddish brown-to-black central spines (only 1 is hooked), surrounded by 18-28 bristle-like spines pressed flat against the stem

Flower: star-shaped pink blossoms form a wreath near the tops of stems; each flower, 1" (2.5 cm) wide, has petals with dark pink stripes and bases surrounding a center of orange male flower parts (anthers) and a green female flower part (stigma)

Blooming: May-June, sometimes in September; about 7-8 days after heavy rainfall; each plant can bloom several times during the summer

Fruit: club-shaped, scarlet red pod, ½-1¼" (1-3 cm) long, is smooth, fleshy, edible and contains small black seeds

densely spiny

Habitat: desert scrub, grasslands and desert mountains from 3,200-4,600' (975-1,400 m); canyons, slopes, flats, beneath shrubs, trees or other cacti; volcanic or limestone soils

Range: western Texas, limited to a couple of counties in the Big Bend area and the Franklin Mountains near El Paso

**Arizona Fishhook
Pincushion**
green stigma

Cob Beehive Cactus
(pg. 127)
white stigma

Cob Beehive Cactus
(pg. 127)
lacks hooked spines

Compare: Although closely related to other species of *Mammillaria* in the state, no other pincushion in Texas has hooked spines. Somewhat similar to Cob Beehive Cactus (pg. 127), which also has pink flowers, but Cob lacks any hooked spines and has a groove on the upper surface of each bump (tubercle), unlike Arizona Fishhook tubercles. When these two cacti are in bloom, compare the stigma color of the pink flowers.

Notes: This small cactus is often overlooked because it usually grows beneath desert shrubs and trees, which provide shelter against sun or frost and protect the cactus from being trampled (nurse plants). In winter, when stems lose water and shrivel, the pincushion is even less noticeable. Gray spines cover the stems, making the plant look more like a rock at first glance. Spines don't entirely cover up the green stems when they swell with summer rainwater. As the pink flowers or red fruit emerge in a ring at the top, the short clumps suddenly become conspicuous.

The longest slender brown central spine in each spine cluster rises above the network of gray radial spines, especially on top of the stem, making the cactus look like a gray pincushion stuck with pins. "Fishhook" is for the thin "pins" that are hooked at the tips. Although the most abundant and widespread pincushion cactus in Arizona (thus the common name), it is restricted in the farthest eastern part of its range to a couple of small areas in Texas.

spines

see page 348 for
larger map

Nellie Beehive Cactus
Coryphantha minima

CYLINDRICAL

**Pineapple
Beehive**

Size: H ½-1" (1-2.5 cm); W ¼-⅔" (.6-1.6 cm)

Shape: tiny round cactus

Stem: single stem, appearing yellowish white and smooth from a distance, but is actually covered with conical bumps (tubercles); each tubercle tipped with white wool and short stout spines; the spines mostly obscure the dark green stem color

Spines: whitish tan or pale yellow with brighter yellow bases; ⅙-¼" (.4-.6 cm) long; some with dark brown tips; aging to gray

Spine Clusters: stubby blunt-tipped spines in clusters; each cluster has 1-4 central spines pressed upward against the stem and a circle of 13-24 radial spines pressed against the stem; radial spines in lower portion of circle are obviously shorter

Flower: magenta flowers at the tip of stem; each bloom, 1" (2.5 cm) wide, has petals with fringed tips; inner petals paler at base; orangish yellow male flower parts (anthers) and a pale green female flower part (stigma)

Blooming: March-June, but mainly April-May

Fruit: round or egg-shaped green pod, up to ¼" (.6 cm) long, sometimes turning yellowish green; fragile dried flower tuft remains attached, but is easily broken off; contains black seeds; ripens 1 month after flowering

Habitat: grasslands from 3,700-4,300' (1,130-1,310 m); in crevices among spike moss on quartz-like rock (novaculite) outcrops

Range: restricted to near Marathon in Brewster County in far western Texas

Nellie Beehive Cactus
stubby, blunt-tipped spines
pressed tightly against
the stem

Hester Beehive Cactus
(pg. 95)
fine, needle-like spines

Davis Hedgehog *(pg. 175)*
sharp spines point
outward

Compare: Mature stems of Hester Beehive Cactus (pg. 95) and Davis Hedgehog (pg. 175) are tiny like Nellie Beehive Cactus stems and occur in the same area. The stubby, blunt-tipped spines pressed against a Nellie Beehive stem are hard to mistake for the needle-like spines of Hester Beehive, which are also pressed against the stem, or the sharp, outward-pointing spines of Davis Hedgehog.

Notes: Measuring less than the width of a quarter, this tiny round cactus is covered with unique spines that are stubby, blunt-tipped and pressed closely against the stem. Once grew near a highway in far western Texas, but that population was wiped out due to intense collecting. Now one of the rarest of cacti, listed in 1979 as endangered by the U.S. Fish and Wildlife Service. In the wild, currently grows in only three sites in Brewster County, Texas. Occurs primarily on private land to which no one is allowed access. Except when blooming, these plants are inconspicuous among spike moss growing among chips of very hard, quartz-like rock (novaculite) and shrink below the soil surface in drought. Single-stemmed in the wild, but branches freely, forming clumps when cultivated.

Available for purchase from specialized nurseries. Easy to cultivate from seed or cuttings, this dwarf cactus is very slow growing, but worth the effort when the relatively large pink flowers appear. The blossoms are easily pollinated by hand, producing fruit with about 30 seeds. Cold hardy to 10°F (-12°C). Place in full sun to light shade and keep dry during the winter.

spines

flower

fruit

CYLINDRICAL

Pineapple Beehive

Duncan Beehive Cactus
Coryphantha duncanii

ee page 348 for larger map

Size: H ⅝-1⅜" (1.5-3.5 cm); W ½-1⅜" (1-3.5 cm)

Shape: round, oval or somewhat conical stem; sometimes branching into 2-3 stems

Stem: single small stem, appearing white and dotted with light brown; overlapping white spines hide the green stem color

Spines: snowy white with light brown bases; tan-to-reddish brown tips on larger spines; ¼-⅝" (.6-1.5 cm) long

Spine Clusters: densely overlapping, bristly spine clusters; each cluster has 4-10 needle-like central spines pressed against the stem (longest one points upward, downward or projects outward) and 20-41 slightly finer radial spines pressed loosely against the stem

Flower: cream-colored flowers at the tip of stem; each bloom, ⅝" (1.5 cm) wide, has long narrow fringed outer petals and 14 inner petals with pinkish or greenish brown midstripes; yellow and white male flower parts (stamens); a green female flower part (stigma)

Blooming: February-March, sometimes blooming again in late summer a week after good rains; opening only on sunny days, closing at night, lasting 2-3 days

Fruit: club-shaped green pod, ½-¾" (1-2 cm) long, turning bright red when ripe with the dried flower tuft breaking off cleanly; contains round black seeds; usually ripens in May

Habitat: desert hills between 2,000-3,700' (610-1,130 m); limestone crevices

Range: Big Bend region of far western Texas

Duncan Beehive Cactus
smaller stems, 1 largest
central spine

Desert Beehive Cactus
(pg. 99)
larger stems, similar-sized
central spines

Golf Ball Pincushion
(pg. 35)
lacks central spines

Compare: Desert Beehive Cactus (pg. 99) can be distinguished from Duncan Beehive Cactus by its somewhat larger stems and similar-sized central spines that point outward and upward, while Duncan has one largest central spine pointing outward and smaller central spines pressed against the stem. The less bristly Golf Ball Pincushion (pg. 35) grows on limestone like Duncan and blooms as early, but Golf Ball Pincushion lacks central spines altogether, has shorter radial spines and much pinker flowers.

Notes: A very small cactus with bristly spines, bright red fruit and cream-colored flowers. The species name *duncanii* is in honor of Frank Duncan, who owned a mine near where the cactus was first discovered. Has slimmer spines than any other beehive cactus except for its two closest relatives, Desert Beehive and Chaffey Beehive Cactus (pg. 107).

Also called Duncan Snowball for its white color and round shape. Difficult to see because it blends into the white background of its home. Restricted to growing deeply seated in cracks in white limestone rocks, unlike the larger Desert Beehive, which is found on flats and bajadas. In fact, some experts think that Duncan is simply a variety of Desert Beehive that is stunted by where it grows. Common in the hottest desert of Big Bend National Park in Texas, but found nowhere else in the world.

spines

flower

fruit

see page 348 for larger map

Junior Tom Thumb Cactus

Coryphantha pottsiana

CYLINDRICAL

Pineapple Beehive

Size: H 1¼-2½" (3-6 cm)

Shape: clumps, 4-40" (10-102 cm) wide, of a few to many bristly stems

Stem: few to numerous round or oval stems, appearing overall rusty reddish brown or sometimes white; each stem, ⅝-1¼" (1.5-3 cm) wide; dense spines obscure the dark green stem color

Spines: white, gray or yellowish tan, often with darker tips; ⅝-⅞" (1.5-2.3 cm) long; outer half of central spines usually bright reddish brown to dark brown

Spine Clusters: fine needle-like spines in clusters; each cluster has 3-10 central spines pointing straight outward, upward or downward, and 21-41 radial spines (1-4 radials are very long, twisted and hair-like)

Flower: rusty orange, orangish yellow or pale green flowers atop stems; each bloom, ½-¾" (1-2 cm) wide, has pointed petals with cream-colored fringed edges, reddish brown midstripes and reddish orange bases; pink and orangish yellow male flower parts (stamens) and a green female flower part (stigma)

Blooming: February-March; opening late morning, closing at night, lasting 6-8 days

Fruit: round or egg-shaped green pod, up to ¾" (2 cm) wide, turns bright red; dried flower tuft remains firmly attached; contains sweet red pulp and brown seeds; ripens 2-3 months after blooming

Habitat: nearly impenetrable thorn scrub between 200-1,000' (60-305 m); among silverleaf bushes; limestone, rocky or silty soils

Range: western border of southern Texas, from near the mouth of the Pecos River extending southeast along the Rio Grande

**Junior Tom Thumb
Cactus**
darker reddish brown
central spines

Sneed Beehive Cactus
(pg. 143)
paler spines; pink flower
with white stigma

Texas Pincushion *(pg. 47)*
all of its radial spines are
hair-like and curly

Compare: Sneed Beehive Cactus (pg. 143) grows in different areas than Junior Tom Thumb Cactus, but it resembles it more than other beehive cacti. Sneed spines are paler than Junior Tom Thumb spines. Sneed has pink, not rusty orange, flowers as in Junior Tom Thumb. Texas Pincushion (pg. 47) grows in some of the same areas as Junior Tom Thumb, but all of its radial spines are hair-like and curly, not just 1-4 of the radial spines that are hair-like in Junior Tom Thumb.

Notes: Junior Tom Thumb forms inconspicuous, but distinctive clumps. The reddish brown outer halves of the central spines can make the mounds appear rust-colored. Sometimes the central spines lack the brown color, thus the clumps look overall white or pale gray. In that case, the round stems help in identification. Easily seen on the western side of International Amistad Reservoir (known as Lake Amistad) in southern Texas. Also found in Mexico.

Although not rare, Junior Tom Thumb is among the many species of beehive cacti threatened by poaching in Texas and Mexico. Cacti are one of the most threatened plant groups in the world. Any disturbance by humans that removes cacti is difficult to overcome because the plants are slow growing and do not reproduce quickly. In addition, small cacti are more affected by climate change due to their long life spans and low reproduction rates. Lengthy droughts of the kind seen in Texas in recent years have had a harsh impact on cacti, even on those that are well adapted to normally arid conditions.

spines

flower

fruit

Whiskerbush Beehive Cactus
Coryphantha ramillosa

see page 348 for larger map

Size: H ½-3½" (1-9 cm); W 1½-3¾" (4-9.5 cm)

Shape: dome-shaped, conical or flat-topped; sometimes branching into a few stems

Stem: compact dark green stem covered with firm conical bumps (tubercles); each tubercle has a groove on upper surface from tip to base and is tipped with shaggy spines; stem color partially visible when plant is well hydrated

Spines: pale yellow or white to dark gray, or reddish brown to dark brown; ½-1¾" (1-4.5 cm) long; often with dark brown-to-black tips

Spine Clusters: long shaggy spines in tangled spine clusters; each cluster has 1 longest needle-like central spine that points straight outward; 2-5 (usually 3) darker, upward-pointing central spines forming a bird's foot pattern; and 13-16 shorter, sometimes twisted radial spines

Flower: pale pink or rosy pink flowers atop stem; each bloom, 1¼-2" (3-5 cm) wide, has long narrow petals and darker pink bases; yellow or orange male flower parts (stamens) and a white female flower part (stigma)

Blooming: August-September, but also in response to rain in other warm months; flowers last 1 day

Fruit: round or pear-shaped, pale-to-dark green pod, ¾" (2 cm) long, with the dried flower tuft remaining firmly attached; sweetly fragrant, juicy pulp is clear or green and contains yellowish brown seeds; usually ripens in November

Habitat: desert scrub from 1,300-3,000' (395-915 m); rocky limestone hilltops and slopes among lechuguillas or creosote bushes, crevices in canyon ledges

Range: Big Bend region of far western Texas

Whiskerbush Beehive Cactus
groove runs the full length of tubercle

Big-needle Beehive Cactus *(pg. 139)*
tubercle groove runs only part of the length

Big-needle Beehive Cactus *(pg. 139)*
larger flower with fringed petals

Compare: The similar but more widespread Big-needle Beehive Cactus (pg. 139) grows as a mound of many stems, as opposed to the single stem of Whiskerbush Beehive Cactus. Big-needle has a groove on each bump (tubercle) that extends only part of the length from the tip toward the base. Big-needle has larger flowers with fringed petals, whereas Whiskerbush petals are not fringed.

Notes: First discovered in 1936 by A. R. Davis, Whiskerbush Beehive Cactus is a small plant with slender spines of various lengths that point out in all directions. Blooms from August through September, but sometimes flowers in April or October, depending upon rains.

The U.S. Fish and Wildlife Service lists this cactus as threatened, thus protecting it under the Endangered Species Act. It is among the cacti in the Center for Plant Conservation's National Collection of Endangered Plants. Luckily, Whiskerbush occurs in Big Bend National Park and on private lands that are relatively safe from poachers. This rare cactus occurs in the wild only in 25 locations near the Lower Canyons along the Rio Grande, a remote region in far western Texas. A few very primitive dirt roads provide limited access into over 160 miles (258 km) of river and surrounding desert. The only corridor to the remainder of the region is the river during high water, which has white-water rapids and whirlpools, and cliffs as tall as 1,000-2,000 feet (305-610 m) along its banks. Sometimes called Big Bend Cory Cactus. Also found in Coahuila, Mexico.

spines

flower

fruit

Missouri Beehive Cactus

Coryphantha missouriensis

see page 349 for
larger map

Size: H 1-3" (2.5-7.5 cm)

Shape: clumps, 6-12" (15-30 cm) wide, of up to 12 round or egg-shaped stems of various sizes, often partially buried; in winter, becomes flat-topped and is mostly underground

Stem: multiple (sometimes single) dark green stems; each stem, ⅞-3" (2.3-7.5 cm) wide, covered with prominent broad conical bumps (tubercles) with grooves on the upper surfaces; each soft tubercle is tipped with short white wool and widely spaced spines; the spines do not hide the stem color

Spines: bright white, pale gray or tan, ⅜-⅔" (.9-1.6 cm) long, aging to gray or yellowish brown; some have tips of dark brownish orange to pale brown

Spine Clusters: widely spaced clusters; each cluster usually lacks central spines (when present, has 1-3 upright central spines with 1 pointing straight outward), but has a circle of 6-20 straight fine radial spines held against the stem

Flower: yellow or salmon-colored flowers at the tips of stems; each bloom, 1⅜-3" (3.5-7.5 cm) wide, has long narrow pointed petals; inner petals with green or rosy pink-to-pale brown midstripes; pink or white, green and yellow flower parts

Blooming: April-June

Fruit: round pod, ½" (1 cm) wide, stays green through the winter, then ripens to scarlet red in the spring, remaining on the plant when blooming resumes; contains tiny black seeds

Habitat: prairies and oak/juniper woodlands from 300-3,000' (90-915 m); limestone hills; water-deposited loamy soils

Range: central and northern Texas

Missouri Beehive Cactus
fine spines, white wool
tipping the tubercles

**Chihuahuan Beehive
Cactus** *(pg. 115)*
stouter spines, white wool
between the tubercles

Longmamma Pincushion
(pg. 59)
light green stem,
slimmer spines

Compare: Chihuahuan Beehive Cactus (pg. 115) resembles Missouri Beehive Cactus, but their ranges do not overlap, thus they are unlikely to be mistaken for each other in the wild. Chihuahuan Beehive has stouter spines and has wool between the bumps (tubercles), while Missouri Beehive has tubercles tipped with white wool. With its long tubercles, Longmamma Pincushion (pg. 59) could be mistaken for Missouri Beehive, but Longmamma has even finer spines than does Missouri.

Notes: A small, clumping cactus with short spines and large tubercles. Often partially buried, thus it is very inconspicuous except when the large, showy flowers are in bloom. Sometimes it looks as if the flowers are sprouting directly from the ground. The resulting fruit ripens to red the following spring when next year's blossoms open. Historically, some Indian tribes of the Great Plains ate the ripe fruit.

Widespread and cold hardy, this cactus is found from North Dakota south to Texas, and in Montana, Wyoming, Colorado, Utah, Arizona and New Mexico. Named in honor of the Missouri River, which is near to where it was discovered. Cacti are found only in the Western Hemisphere and, surprisingly, are native to every state in this country except Vermont and Maine. While thought of as desert plants, cacti also grow in grasslands, meadows, on seashores or atop mountains.

spines

flower

see page 349 for larger map

CYLINDRICAL

Pineapple
Beehive

Grooved Beehive Cactus
Coryphantha sulcata

Size: H 1½-3" (4-7.5 cm)

Shape: clumps, up to 24" (61 cm) wide, of dozens of round or egg-shaped stems of varying sizes; often flat-topped

Stem: single or multiple dark green stems; each stem, 2½-3" (6-7.5 cm) wide, is covered with prominent broad conical bumps (tubercles) with grooves on the upper surfaces; each soft tubercle is tipped with short white wool and widely spaced, stout spines; the spines do not obscure the stem color

Spines: yellowish or pinkish white, becoming gray to nearly white, ⅜-⅔" (.9-1.6 cm) long, with dark reddish brown or black tips

Spine Clusters: widely spaced clusters; each cluster has 1-4 stout upright central spines pressed against the stem (stoutest one points straight outward or curves downward) and a circle of 8-15 radial spines that are straight or slightly curved toward the stem; sometimes lacks central spines

Flower: dark golden yellow flowers with red centers, at the tips of stems; each bloom, 1⅜-3" (3.5-7.5 cm) wide, has pointed petals with red bases, and red and yellow flower parts

Blooming: April-May, maybe again sporadically in summer

Fruit: broadly oval, slimy green pod, ⅝-1⅜" (1.5-3.5 cm) long, turns yellowish green when ripe with dried flower tuft remaining attached; contains comma-shaped, shiny, reddish brown seeds; ripens 3-4 months after blooming

western form

immature plant lacks central spines

Habitat: grasslands, shrubby thickets and savannahs from 300-2,000' (90-610 m); under junipers, oaks or bushes; gravelly, clay or sandy soils

Range: central and southwestern Texas, in a broad area from north of Fort Worth, south through Austin, to the southwestern border of the state; also an isolated area in southern Texas

Grooved Beehive Cactus
central spines point out
and curve slightly down-
ward, tubercles visible

**Sea Urchin Beehive
Cactus** (pg. 111)
tubercles entirely obscured
by spines

Missouri Beehive Cactus
(pg. 87)
central spines
point upward

Compare: In the western portion of its range, Grooved Beehive Cactus is a single-stemmed plant closely resembling Sea Urchin Beehive (pg. 111), but the bumps (tubercles) of Grooved are visible, unlike those of Sea Urchin. East of Austin, Grooved looks much like a multiple-stemmed, dark green Missouri Beehive Cactus (pg. 87), but Missouri has overall slimmer spines and upward-pointing central spines, while the stout centrals of Grooved are slightly curved.

Notes: In the drier, western portion of its range, Grooved Beehive Cactus is a small cactus with a single stem. In the moister, eastern part of its range, it branches with age into many stems of different sizes. This cactus has barely overlapping spine clusters, each with a single, stout, outward-pointing central spine. Immature plants lack central spines. Species name *sulcata*, from the Latin word for "furrow," refers to the groove on the upper surface of each tubercle. The grooves are more visible in this member of the *Coryphantha* genus than it is in most other beehive cacti, since the tubercles are not hidden by the spines. Also called Nipple Cactus.

Grown by cactus enthusiasts in Eurasia and Europe for its attractive, red-throated yellow flowers. Although Grooved is found elsewhere in Texas, illegal trade of cacti native to the Chihuahuan Desert, which extends into Mexico, threatens extinction of many beautiful cacti. Home to about 684 cactus species, Mexico has the highest concentration of cacti in the world. Sadly, around 35 species of beehive cacti are regularly illegally collected from Mexico and sold abroad.

spines

see page 349 for
larger map

Hester Beehive Cactus
Coryphantha hesteri

CYLINDRICAL

**Pineapple
Beehive**

Size: H 2-3½" (5-9 cm)

Shape: dense clumps, up to 12" (30 cm) wide, of round or conical (sometimes flat-topped) stems; partly buried in soil so only top half is visible

Stem: single or multiple stems, ⅝-2" (1.5-5 cm) wide, light green, covered with prominent conical bumps (tubercles); each tubercle has groove on upper surface and tipped with spine clusters; stem color is easily seen if the plant is well hydrated

Spines: white or yellow with reddish brown or black tips, ⅜-⅔" (.9-1.6 cm) long, turning gray with age

Spine Clusters: 13-18 spines in clusters; each cluster lacks central spines, but has 9-13 longer, closely spaced radial spines in the upper part of the cluster pointing upward in a tuft; remainder of spines in a semicircle in lower part of cluster

Flower: rosy pink or magenta flowers at the tips of stems; each bloom, ⅝-¾" (1.5-2 cm) wide, has backward-curving petals with paler edges and fringed tips, around pink and orangish yellow flower parts

Blooming: April-June, may bloom again sporadically until November, but only about 1 week after a good rain; opens about noon, closes in late afternoon

Fruit: round or egg-shaped green pod, ⅕-⅓" (.5-.8 cm) long, occasionally turning reddish green when ripe; dried flower tuft remains in place; contains round dark brown seeds; usually ripens August-October

Habitat: grasslands and oak/juniper woodlands from 3,600-5,300' (1,100-1,615 m); dry hillsides, bajadas, crevices in rocks, quartz-like rock (novaculite) outcrops; limestone soils

Range: Big Bend region of far western Texas

Hester Beehive Cactus
tubercles visible, tuft of closely spaced spines point upward

Common Beehive Cactus *(pg. 123)*
tubercles partly hidden, central spines point out

Whiskerbush Beehive Cactus *(pg. 83)*
pink flower with white stigma

Compare: Common Beehive Cactus (pg. 123) resembles Hester Beehive Cactus, but all its parts (stem, flowers, fruit and spines) are larger, and the spines partially hide the bumps (tubercles). Also, Hester has clusters of all-radial spines, while each Common spine cluster has a central spine that points straight outward. The rosy pink flowers of Whiskerbush Beehive Cactus (pg. 83) look much like Hester blooms, but Hester flowers have pink female flower parts (stigmas), while stigmas in Whiskerbush blossoms are white.

Notes: A small, round or slightly conical cactus with relatively large conical tubercles on the stem. Each tubercle is tipped with a cluster of spines that have an unusual arrangement–the longest spines are grouped together at top of each cluster and form a tuft. The stems withdraw to ground level or into rock crevices during drought and are usually covered with grass, making them nearly impossible to spot.

Found only in Texas, the species name honors J. P. Hester, who discovered this cactus in the 1930s. Hester Beehive Cactus is one of the many dwarf cacti found in the Chihuahuan Desert region, home to about a quarter of the estimated 1,500 cactus species in the world.

spines

flower

fruit

see page 349 for larger map

Desert Beehive Cactus
Coryphantha dasyacantha

CYLINDRICAL

Pineapple
Beehive

Size: H 1¾-4" (4.5-10 cm); W 1-1¾" (2.5-4.5 cm)

Shape: round stem, becoming conical with age; rarely branching into 2-5 stems

Stem: single stem appearing white; overlapping white spines hide the green stem color

Spines: white, translucent straw-colored, or pinkish brown with reddish brown-to-nearly black tips; ¼-⅔" (.6-1.6 cm) long

Spine Clusters: densely overlapping, bristly spine clusters; each cluster has 4-9 pinkish brown, needle-like central spines that point outward and upward, and 21-31 finer, shorter, white radial spines pressed loosely against the stem

Flower: small salmon-colored or brownish green blooms at the tip of stem; each funnel-shaped flower, ⅝" (1.5 cm) wide, has fringed outer petals, 14 inner petals with pinkish or greenish brown midstripes, yellow and white male flower parts (stamens) and a green female flower part (stigma)

Blooming: March-July, sometimes blooming again in late summer after good rains; opening midday, closing at night, lasting 2-3 days

Fruit: somewhat dry, club-shaped pod, ½-1" (1-2.5 cm) long, green, turning bright red with dried flower tuft remaining attached, containing round black seeds; ripens 1½-2½ months after blooming

Habitat: desert scrub, grasslands and oak/juniper woodlands from 2,500-5,500' (760-1,675 m); flats or gravel bajadas, among creosote bushes, mesquite trees or lechuguillas; volcanic or limestone, rocky or silty soils

Range: scattered areas in far western Texas

Desert Beehive Cactus
dried flower tufts remain
on fruit

Duncan Beehive Cactus
(pg. 75)
fruit does not have dried
flower tufts attached

Sneed Beehive Cactus
(pg. 143)
single-stemmed plant
looks like Desert Beehive

Compare: Duncan Beehive Cactus (pg. 75) is hard to distinguish from Desert Beehive Cactus, except when fruit is present. Duncan fruit does not have an attached dried flower tuft like the tuft that remains on Desert fruit. Single-stemmed plants of Sneed Beehive Cactus (pg. 143) can look much like Desert, but Sneed usually branches into many stems.

Notes: The species name *dasyacantha*, meaning "shaggy-spined," describes the overall appearance of this plant. Sometimes known as Big Bend Foxtail Cactus. Rare throughout its range in the Chihuahuan Desert and once thought to grow wild only in Texas and Mexico. Now known to occur in one site in southern New Mexico that contains rare cacti.

About 70 species of cacti ranging from Canada to Mexico to Cuba are classified as members of the genus *Coryphantha*, with more than a dozen species found in Texas. The genus name is derived from two Greek words combined to mean "summit flower," referring to the location of the blooms on the tops of the stems. All cacti in this genus have a lengthwise groove on top of each bump (tubercle), but the tubercles are not visible in this species.

This cactus is easy to cultivate. Plant in gravelly soil with good drainage in a location with full sun to light shade. Prone to rot, so in summer give it water when soil is completely dry–do not water at all in winter. Cold hardy to 10°F (-12°C).

spines

flower

fruit

Pineapple
Beehive

Lloyd Pineapple Cactus
Echinomastus mariposensis

ee page 349 for
larger map

Size: H 1-4¾" (2.5-12 cm); W 1-2½" (2.5-6 cm)

Shape: short round or cylindrical cactus

Stem: single bluish green stem with 21 low ribs arranged in spirals and lined with short bumps (tubercles); each tubercle tipped with dense spine clusters that totally obscure the stem color

Spines: ashy white; largest spines often tipped bluish gray, bluish black or brown; ⅙-¾" (.4-2 cm) long

Spine Clusters: overlapping and interlacing tangled clusters; each cluster has 4 (rarely 6) central spines (3 largest are chalky blue and pointing upward, 1 shorter is curving downward) and 19-32 radial spines pressed loosely against the stem; shorter radials are noticeably slimmer than central spines

Flower: yellowish white flowers in a tuft at the top of stem; each funnel-shaped blossom, ¾-1½" (2-4 cm) wide, has petals with dull pinkish or greenish brown mid-stripes, yellow male flower parts (stamens) and a green female flower part (stigma)

Blooming: February-March; opening about 1 o'clock in the afternoon, closing at night, lasting 3-4 days

Fruit: round or oblong green pod, 1" (2.5 cm) long, drying and becoming papery thin, and either remaining intact or splitting open irregularly, releasing seeds; ripens in April

Habitat: desert scrub between 2,500-3,700' (760-1,130 m); lime-stone gravel ridges, mesas

Range: Big Bend region in far western Texas

Lloyd Pineapple Cactus
looks similar to Rattail
Pincushion

Rattail Pincushion *(pg. 63)*
multiple-stemmed, with
more numerous central
and radial spines

Cob Beehive Cactus
(pg. 127)
when single-stemmed,
resembles Lloyd

Compare: The ashy white appearance and upward-curving central spines tipped with reddish brown or bluish gray make Rattail Pincushion (pg. 63) look similar to Lloyd Pineapple Cactus. Rattail usually is multiple-stemmed with 6-12 central and 37-49 radial spines, unlike the single-stemmed Lloyd, which has fewer central and radial spines. When not flowering, Cob Beehive Cactus (pg. 127) can also be mistaken for Lloyd, but typically is multiple-stemmed.

Notes: About the size of a golf or tennis ball, this single-stemmed cactus has slim white radial spines so dense they cover up the bluish green stem. The overall white appearance is broken by scattered, upward-pointing, dark central spines–those on top of the cactus are tipped bluish gray, while those on the sides of the stem are brown-tipped. Radial spines pressing against the stem in older clusters are horizontal to the ground. Produces blooms in late winter or early spring, earlier than most cacti.

Prefers a rockier habitat than any other pineapple cactus. Blends into the blindingly white background of the barren limestone hillsides upon which it grows. Closely related to Warnock Pineapple Cactus (pg. 131), but the two species are not found growing together. Lloyd grows only on limestone, while Warnock is found in a wider variety of soil types.

Although common in the limited area of Texas where it occurs, conservationists are still concerned about Lloyd's survival because of its restricted range. Also found in Coahuila, Mexico.

spines

immature fruit

ee page 349 for
larger map

**Pineapple
Beehive**

Chaffey Beehive Cactus
Coryphantha chaffeyi

Size: H 2-4¼" (5-10.5 cm); W 1¼-1¾" (3-4.5 cm)

Shape: round stem, becoming short cylindrical with age; sometimes branching into 2-3 stems

Stem: single stem appearing white; overlapping white spines hide the green stem color

Spines: snowy white, or translucent with light gray bases; sometimes with pale yellow-to-red tips; ¼-⅝" (.6-1.5 cm) long

Spine Clusters: densely overlapping, slightly bristly spine clusters; each cluster has 8-10 needle-like central spines pressed tightly against the stem (longest one points outward, upward or downward) and 20-40 slightly finer radial spines pressed against the stem

Flower: orange or salmon-colored flowers at tip of stem; each bloom, ⅜" (.9 cm) wide, has pointed narrow petals, inner cream petals with broad orange or salmon-colored midstripes; flower parts are pink, yellow and green

Blooming: March-May; opening at noon, closing at night, lasting 2-6 days

Fruit: oval or club-shaped green pod, ½-¾" (1-2 cm) long, turning bright red when ripe with the dried flower tuft breaking off cleanly, containing dark brown-to-black seeds; ripens 1-3 months after blooming

Habitat: oak/juniper woodlands from 4,700-7,300' (1,435-2,225 m); among rocks and grasses on open slopes on mountains; volcanic and limestone soils

Range: restricted to the Chisos Mountains of Big Bend National Park in far western Texas

Chaffey Beehive Cactus
more and slimmer
snowy white spines

Desert Beehive Cactus
(pg. 99)
fewer and thicker spines

Cob Beehive Cactus
(pg. 127)
spines of various colors

Compare: Desert Beehive Cactus (pg. 99) can be distinguished from Chaffey Beehive Cactus by its fewer and thicker spines and, when in bloom, by its larger flowers. Cob Beehive Cactus (pg. 127) sometimes grows at the same high elevations as Chaffey. Lengthening with age into a cylindrical shape, Cob begins life as a round plant like Chaffey, but Cob has spines of various colors, unlike the mostly snowy white spines of Chaffey.

Notes: Mainly a Mexican species that crosses the border into the United States only in Big Bend National Park, this small cactus has slightly bristly spines, bright red fruit and orange or salmon-colored flowers. Also called Biscuit Cactus for its shape. The species name *chaffeyi* is in honor of Elswood Chaffey, who was the first to collect this cactus in Mexico in the early 1900s.

Found in the Chisos Mountains, whereas its closest relatives, Duncan Beehive Cactus (pg. 75) and Desert Beehive Cactus, are found in the lower deserts. Chaffey has at times been considered a variety of Desert. Chaffey is propagated on a 507-acre (203 ha) nature center south of Fort Davis, Texas, through the efforts of the Chihuahuan Desert Research Institute. Cacti and succulents grown there are sold to the public annually.

spines

flower

fruit

see page 350 for
larger map

CYLINDRICAL

Pineapple
Beehive

Sea Urchin Beehive Cactus

Coryphantha echinus

Size: H 1-6" (2.5-15 cm)

Shape: large clumps, 12-32" (30-80 cm) wide, with 15-50 round stems of various ages; may become conical with age

Stem: single or multiple stems appearing gray or yellowish tan; each stem, 1-3" (2.5-7.5 cm) wide; thick interlocking spines obscure the green stem color

Spines: whitish to dark gray, or brownish red to yellowish tan; ½-1" (1-2.5 cm) long; with dark brown tips

Spine Clusters: densely overlapping spine clusters; each cluster has 3-7 central spines pressed against the stem (longest one points straight outward or curves downward) and a circle of 16-27 radial spines slightly curving against the stem

Flower: glossy, pale yellow flowers at the tip of stem; each large showy bloom, 1-2½" (2.5-6 cm) wide, has long wedge-tipped petals around reddish orange and yellow flower parts

Blooming: April-July; opening fully by noon, lasting only 1-2 hours

Fruit: slimy oval green pod, ½-1" (1-2.5 cm) long, turns dull yellowish green when ripe with dried flower tuft remaining attached; contains shiny, comma-shaped, reddish brown seeds; ripens 3-4 months after blooming

immature plant lacks
central spines

Habitat: desert scrub and grasslands between 1,000-4,800' (305-1,465 m); plateaus, mountains, arroyos, on limestone slopes, near volcanic ridges, among creosote bushes

Range: far western Texas plus an area east of and bordering the Pecos River, and a tiny area in the west central part of the state

Sea Urchin Beehive Cactus
many radial spines obscure the stem

Grooved Beehive Cactus *(pg. 91)*
fewer radial spines do not conceal the green stem

Glory-of-Texas *(pg. 171)*
immature plant has tangled radial spines

Compare: The related Grooved Beehive Cactus (pg. 91) resembles Sea Urchin Beehive Cactus, but Grooved has fewer radial spines, which allows the green stem color to show, while the many radial spines of Sea Urchin hide the green stem. Immature plants of Glory-of-Texas (pg. 171) also can be mistaken for Sea Urchin, but its spine clusters look messier than those of Sea Urchin.

Notes: A single round stem of this cactus looks much like a sea urchin, as the plant is covered with interlocking stout spines and has one outward-pointing central spine in each spine cluster. In fact, the species name *echinus* is derived from the Greek word for "sea urchin." One of two varieties in the state, this form usually remains as a single stem with whitish gray spines and is more widespread, occurring throughout western Texas on both sides of the Pecos River.

Another variety, found near the Rio Grande in the Big Bend region, forms large clumps of stems and has dark gray-to-nearly black spines. Develops outward-pointing central spines when young, and the stems become conical with age. Immature plants of both varieties lack projecting central spines.

The showy flowers are large for the stem size. Blooms are only open 1-2 hours at midday, lasting for just one day. This is an unusually short period of time for a cactus to bloom. Although found in the hottest deserts, Sea Urchin is cold hardy to -20°F (-29°C).

spines

flower

fruit

Chihuahuan Beehive Cactus
Neolloydia conoidea

Pineapple Beehive

see page 350 for larger map

Size: H 2-6" (5-15 cm)

Shape: clumps of round or slender cylindrical stems

Stem: grayish or yellowish green stems, 1-2½" (2.5-6 cm) wide, with prominent soft conical bumps (tubercles) in 8-13 spiraling rows; each tubercle has a woolly groove on the upper side and is tipped with spines; much white wool packed between tubercles at the top of stem; the stem color is partially visible

Spines: white to gray with dark tips, or all dark brown or black; ¼-1" (.6-2.5 cm) long

Spine Clusters: widely spaced clusters; each cluster has 1-6 (usually 2-4) stout upright central spines (longest one is black and points straight outward, or curves downward or upward) and a circle of 14-17 straight grayish white radial spines; can lack central spines

Flower: rosy pink flowers atop stems; each bloom, 1¼-2¼" (3-5.5 cm) wide, with magenta inner petals; yellow and white flower parts can appear pink due to reflection from the inner petals

Blooming: March-August, but mainly May-June; opens mid-morning, closes by midafternoon, lasts 1-3 days

Fruit: cylindrical green pod, ⅝-1⅜" (1.5-3.5 cm) long, turning pinkish white with the dried flower tuft breaking off; dries to papery tan and opens along vertical slits, releasing black or gray seeds; ripens in November

variety lacking
central spines

Habitat: desert scrub, thorn scrub and desert mountains from 1,500-4,000' (460-1,220 m); rocky limestone soils

Range: far western Texas

Chihuahuan Beehive Cactus
shorter spines

Big-needle Beehive Cactus *(pg. 139)*
longer spines, sometimes twisted

Whiskerbush Beehive Cactus *(pg. 83)*
longer spines

Compare: Chihuahuan Beehive Cactus resembles Big-needle Beehive Cactus (pg. 139) and Whiskerbush Beehive Cactus (pg. 83), both of which are in the genus *Coryphantha*. Big-needle and Whiskerbush have much longer spines and larger flowers than does Chihuahuan. The spines of Big-needle are also sometimes twisted.

Notes: A small cylindrical, very slender cactus with straight, needle-like spines that only partially hide the stem color and the prominent bumps (tubercles) spiraling in rows around the stem. The genus name *conoidea* is derived from the Greek word meaning "a type of cone," and probably refers to the cone-shaped tubercles. Also known as Texas Cone Cactus. The rosy pink flowers and the fruit emerge from the eye-catching, plentiful white wool on top of the stems. In the wild, Chihuahuan Beehive Cactus is found only in Texas and northern Mexico, and it is abundant in some locations.

This cactus can have spines sticking straight outward from each of the spine clusters, making the plant look spiny, or it can lack central spines altogether. That form, with only radial spines arranged in a circular pattern and pressed closely to the stem, is not very prickly when handled.

tubercle groove   fruit

see page 350 for larger map

Pineapple Beehive

Robust-spine Beehive Cactus
Coryphantha robustispina

Size: H 2-6" (5-15 cm); W 2-3½" (5-9 cm)

Shape: low-growing cactus, beehive-shaped or round with a flat top; rarely branching

Stem: single grayish green stem covered with large thick conical bumps (tubercles), each with an obvious groove on the upper surface and tipped with a stout spine cluster that does not cover up the stem color

Spines: pale yellow, gray or brown, with dark tips; ½-1⅜" (1-3.5 cm) long

Spine Clusters: 1-4 stout central spines that are straight, hooked or curved, are surrounded by a circle of 6-16 thick radial spines

Flower: frilly, pale yellow flowers in a dense cluster at the top of stem; each blossom, 2-2½" (5-6 cm) wide, has long slender petals with bronze bases around a yellow center; bloom held partially closed by the spines

Blooming: April-June, then again July-September following warm summer rains; flowers last only 1 day

Fruit: juicy cone-shaped green pod, 1½-2" (4-5 cm) long, remaining green when ripe; flower tuft breaks off cleanly; fruit hidden by spines and often mistaken for a tubercle; ripens 2-3 months after blooming

Habitat: desert scrub, grasslands and oak/juniper woodlands from 2,700-5,200' (825-1,585 m); bajadas, grassy hills, valleys, among creosote bushes or saltbushes; sandy or silty soils deposited by water runoff of limestone or volcanic rock

Range: far western Texas

Robust-spine Beehive Cactus
cone-shaped tubercles and smooth spines

Horse Crippler *(pg. 163)*
stem has ribs, not separate tubercles

Horse Crippler *(pg. 163)*
pink, not yellow, flowers

Compare: A small Horse Crippler plant (pg. 163) can superficially resemble Robust-spine Beehive Cactus, but has vertical folds (ribs) in the stem and flattened central spines with horizontal ridges, unlike the separate, cone-shaped bumps (tubercles) and smooth, needle-shaped spines of Robust-spine. Easy to identify when in bloom, Horse Crippler flowers are pink, not yellow.

Notes: Robust-spine Beehive Cactus has stouter spines than any other beehive cacti, looking almost like a tiny barrel cactus. Species name *robustispina* is for its thick, rigid spines. Also called Devil's Pincushion. The wide tubercles that show through the spines resemble the skin of a pineapple. Called by another name, Pineapple Cactus, for this characteristic. New plants emerge from the tubercles of the older plants.

Blooms multiple times, in spring and then again in summer after warm rains. Its bronze-tinged, pale yellow flowers cannot open fully because the spines get in the way. Cone-shaped fruit form several months after flowering and stay green, looking like additional tubercles. The fruit is very fragrant, smelling much like a tropical mango or banana.

Also found in Arizona, southern New Mexico and northern Mexico. Although sometimes common in an area, in many places the plants are low in density, with only 1-2 growing in each location. Listed as endangered, thus protected under the Endangered Species Act.

spines

immature fruit

CYLINDRICAL

Pineapple Beehive

Common Beehive Cactus
Coryphantha vivipara

see page 350 for larger map

Size: H 1-8" (2.5-20 cm); W 1-4½" (2.5-11 cm)

Shape: low-growing round or cylindrical cactus with a flat top, or branching into a few or many stems; in winter, becomes more flat-topped and may be over halfway underground

Stem: single or multiple (up to 30) green stems, each covered with spirals of large conical bumps (tubercles) grooved on upper surface and tipped with overlapping spines that partially obscure the stem color

Spines: white, pinkish gray or reddish brown; some with dark reddish brown tips; ³⁄₁₀-1" (.7-2.5 cm) long

Spine Clusters: 4-14 rigid central spines that point outward, upward and downward, and a circle of 10-40 stiff needle-like radial spines pressed closely against the stem

Flower: frilly pink or magenta flowers in a dense bouquet at the top of stem; each bloom, 1-2½" (2.5-6 cm) wide, has pink-to-white and yellow male flower parts (anthers) and a white female flower part (stigma)

Blooming: May-June, sometimes again in late summer after good rains; opening midday, closing at night

Fruit: juicy green pod, ½-1" (1-2.5 cm) long, remaining green but tinged with purplish marks when ripe, containing reddish brown seeds; ripens 2-5 months after flowering

Habitat: desert scrub, basin grasslands and woodlands from 1,000-5,000' (305-1,525 m); rocky slopes, mountains, open areas; among grasses, mesquite and prickly pear cacti; volcanic or water-deposited soils

Range: far western, west central and northwestern Texas

Common Beehive Cactus
tubercles not in
vertical rows

**Woven-spine Pineapple
Cactus** (pg. 135)
tubercles in vertical rows

Cob Beehive Cactus
(pg. 127)
young plant looks similar
to Common Beehive

Compare: While similar in appearance, Woven-spine Pineapple Cactus (pg. 135) has bumps (tubercles) in vertical rows, unlike the tubercle spirals of Common Beehive. Young rounded plants of Cob Beehive Cactus (pg. 127) look much like Common Beehive. However, the spine clusters of older Cob Beehive fall off the tubercles at the bases of the cylindrical stems, leaving corncob-like knobs. The spine clusters remain on Common Beehive stems.

Notes: Aptly named for its abundance, this is the most widespread and plentiful cactus in its genus. *Coryphantha*, meaning "summit flower," refers to the placement of the blooms. *Vivipara*, Latin for "sprouting from the parent plant," is for the production of new buds on old stems that drop off and become new plants.

Beehive cacti are similar to pincushion cacti, differing by flower location, spine thickness, presence of tubercle grooves and taproot length. Common Beehive has a bouquet of flowers blooming at the tip of the stem, rather than in a ring at the edge of the stem top as in pincushion cacti. This cactus is sometimes called Spiny Star for its spines, which, like most beehive cactus spines, are thicker than the fine spines of pincushion cacti. The upper surface of each beehive tubercle has a groove, which pincushion tubercles lack.

Ranges as far west as Nevada and as far east as Oklahoma, and from northern Mexico to Canada. Extremely cold hardy to -8°F (-22°C) and one of only four cactus species that grows in Canada.

spines

flower

fruit

Cob Beehive Cactus
Coryphantha tuberculosa

ee page 350 for larger map

Size: H 2-7" (5-18 cm)

Shape: clumps of 3-50 stems, with a mix of young small round stems and mature cylindrical pointed stems; sometimes a single large stem

Stem: single or multiple stems, each 1-2½" (2.5-6 cm) wide, appearing gray or brown; covered with spirals of hard conical bumps (tubercles) grooved on upper surface and tipped with overlapping spines partially obscuring the green stem color; tubercles at bases of older stems lack spines and look like corncobs

Spines: white, pale gray or tan; ¼-⅝" (.6-1.6 cm) long; largest are tipped with pinkish gray or reddish tan

Spine Clusters: densely overlapping spine clusters; each cluster has 1-2 stouter inner central spines pointing straight outward, 3 central spines pointing upward against the stem in a bird's foot pattern and 15-25 light gray radial spines pressed loosely against the stem

Flower: pale pink flowers at the tips of stems; each blossom, ¾-1¾" (2-4.5 cm) wide, has fringed outer petals, inner petals with darker bases, pale yellowish white male flower parts (stamens) and a white female flower part (stigma)

Blooming: April-August, after rainstorms in late summer; opening late afternoon, staying open until after dusk, closing late at night, lasting 2 or more days

Fruit: narrowly egg-shaped green pod, ½-1" (1-2.5 cm) long, turning bright red; dried flower tuft remains attached; contains reddish brown seeds

Habitat: desert and mountain grasslands, and oak/juniper woodlands from 1,700-6,700' (520-2,045 m); rock crevices, ridges, slopes, among creosote bushes or lechuguillas; volcanic rocky soils or limestone soils

Range: far western Texas

Cob Beehive Cactus
inner petals lack dark
midstripes, flower has
a white stigma

Desert Beehive Cactus
(pg. 99)
midstripes on petals,
flower has a green stigma

Desert Beehive Cactus
(pg. 99)
whiter spines totally
obscure stem color

Compare: Desert Beehive Cactus (pg. 99) may be difficult to distinguish from Cob Beehive Cactus, except when fruit or flowers are present. Desert flower petals have midstripes, while Cob petals are solid-colored with darker bases. Desert flowers have green female flower parts (stigmas), not white stigmas as in Cob blooms. The paler-appearing stem of Desert also has whiter spines than Cob.

Notes: Cob Beehive Cactus forms irregular clumps of various-sized stems that appear gray when growing in soils derived from limestone, while plants found on volcanic rocky ground grow as single stems that look reddish brown. The spine clusters drop off the bumps (tubercles) on the bases of older Cob Beehive stems, leaving corncob-like knobs. Species name *tuberculosa*, derived from Latin words meaning "full of knobs," refers to this knobby appearance.

Blooms in late afternoon and evening (later in the day than other beehive cacti), and its inner petals lack the darker midstripes of most beehive cactus flowers. These large, widely spreading, pale blossoms are distinctive, making this cactus easy to identify when blooming.

Over half the cacti in Texas can be found in the 16 counties either west of or bordering the eastern bank of the Pecos River. Cob Beehive is one of the most common cacti in this far western region of the state, occurring from the cliffs along the Rio Grande to the upper elevations of the mountains. Also found in New Mexico and northern Mexico.

spines

flower

immature fruit

Warnock Pineapple Cactus

Echinomastus warnockii

see page 350 for larger map

Size: H 1½-8" (4-20 cm); W 1-2½" (2.5-6 cm)

Shape: round or cylindrical cactus, usually low growing

Stem: single whitish green stem with 13 low ribs arranged in spirals and lined with short bumps (tubercles); each tubercle tipped with spreading spine clusters that do not hide the stem

Spines: tan to pale gray, pinkish or yellowish brown (rarely dull white); usually with pale gray or bluish gray tips; ⅓-1" (.8-2.5 cm) long

Spine Clusters: overlapping and interlacing tangled clusters; each cluster has 1-4 central spines (1 pointing outward and the rest pointing upward and pressed against radial spines) and 11-17 rigid straight radial spines pressed loosely against the stem; radials only slightly slimmer than central spines

Flower: white flowers in dense tuft at top of stem; each wide open blossom, 1" (2.5 cm) wide, has petals with faint midstripes (outer petals curve backward), pale green and orangish yellow male flower parts (stamens) and a green female flower part (stigma)

Blooming: February-March, over a period of several weeks; opening just after noon, closing at night, lasting 2-5 days

Fruit: round light green pod, 1" (2.5 cm) long, turning pinkish green when mature, drying and becoming papery thin, splitting irregularly lengthwise, releasing seeds; ripens May-July

Habitat: desert scrub between 1,900-4,500' (580-1,370 m); gravel ridges, bajadas, arroyos, limestone hills, gypsum flats, among sparse grasses and creosote bushes or dense scrub

Range: far western Texas

Warnock Pineapple Cactus
central and radial spines similar; stem color shows

Lloyd Pineapple Cactus
(pg. 103)
ashy white radial spines totally obscure stem color

Lloyd Pineapple Cactus
(pg. 103)
central spines markedly stouter than radials

Compare: The similar and closely related Lloyd Pineapple Cactus (pg. 103) occurs in the Big Bend area like Warnock Pineapple Cactus, but the two species grow in different soil types. There is little size difference between the central and radial spines of Warnock, while the untidy-looking Lloyd has more radial spines that are much slimmer than its central spines. Spines totally cover the Lloyd stem color, while spines allow the whitish green stem to be partially visible in Warnock.

Notes: Six species occur in the genus *Echinomastus* in the Southwest. Warnock Pineapple Cactus is found only in Texas in the United States, but also occurs in northern Mexico. The genus name is derived from Greek words for "spiny breast," referring to the numerous spines tipping each bump (tubercle). These cacti are most closely related to the fishhook cacti, which differ by having one hooked central spine. Pineapple cacti have straight or curving (not hooked) central spines. Species name *warnockii* is for the renowned botanist Barton H. Warnock, a leading authority on the plants of far western Texas.

Abundant and common in the Big Bend area, Warnock blooms in late winter to early spring, earlier than most other cacti. Pollinated by bees, beetles and other insects. It is usually seen as a single stem, but older plants can produce a short branch at the base and develop more ribs, numbering over 20. Immature plants begin with a single central spine, growing up to four central spines as they age.

spines

immature fruit

CYLINDRICAL

Woven-spine Pineapple Cactus
Echinomastus intertextus

Pineapple Beehive

ee page 351 for
larger map

Size: H 2-8" (5-20 cm); W 1-4" (2.5-10 cm)

Shape: low-growing round or cylindrical cactus

Stem: single dull green stem with 11-13 wide vertical ribs lined with spine clusters; ribs twist around the stem as the cactus elongates with age

Spines: white to straw-colored with pink or dull red tips; 1/5-1" (.5-2.5 cm) long; aging to gray

Spine Clusters: interlacing, spider-like clusters; each cluster has 1-2 long central spines pointing upward, 1 shorter outward-pointing central spine and 13-25 stiff, slightly inward-curving radial spines pressed closely against the stem or spreading up and out

Flower: 4-7 coconut-scented, pale pink flowers in a dense cluster at the top of stem; each blossom, 1-1⅜" (2.5-3.5 cm) wide, has brown midstripes on outside of petals, pale yellow male flower parts (stamens) and a red, pink or white female flower part (stigma)

Blooming: February-April; opening just before noon, closing at night, lasting 3 days

Fruit: round green pod, ⅝" (1.5 cm) long, turning dull pink, then drying and turning to tan when mature, releasing seeds through a pore at the base; ripens 1-2 months after flowering

prickly variety

wide ribs

immature plant

Habitat: grasslands and grassy areas in mountain woodlands (sometimes with oaks and junipers) between 3,000-5,800' (915-1,770 m); ridges, grassy slopes, bajadas, hidden under shrubs or grasses, often among volcanic rocks

Range: far western Texas

Woven-spine Pineapple Cactus
pink-tinged, red-tipped spines and green stems

Warnock Pineapple Cactus *(pg. 131)*
whitish green stem; bluish gray spines

Warnock Pineapple Cactus *(pg. 131)*
orangish yellow stamens and a green stigma

Compare: While resembling the prickly variety of Woven-spine, Warnock Pineapple Cactus (pg. 131) has whitish green stems and bluish gray spines, not green stems and pink-tipped spines like Woven-spine. Also unlike Woven-spine, which has pale yellow male flower parts (stamens) and red, pink or white female flower parts (stigmas), Warnock has orangish yellow stamens and green stigmas.

Notes: The most common pineapple cactus in far western Texas, this small, single-stemmed cactus is easily overlooked since it is often hidden by grasses. Young stems are flat-topped and round, growing more cylindrical with age. The radial spines are pinkish white and red-tipped. Central spines are pink to dull gray. The more common variety of this cactus has central and inward-curving radial spines, most of which are pressed closely against the stem, making it look like the cactus can be handled with bare hands without being stuck. The prickly variety in the Franklin Mountains near El Paso has its radial and central spines spreading in all directions.

One of the earliest flowering cacti in Texas, sometimes blooming in February, but more commonly in March and April. Pale pink flowers are large and showy. Fruit develops in April through June, drying and turning tan.

Grows as a single cactus or in scattered colonies in Texas, Arizona, New Mexico and the Mexican states of Chihuahua and Sonora. Sometimes called Chihuahuan Pineapple Cactus.

spines

flower

fruit

Pineapple
Beehive

Big-needle Beehive Cactus
Coryphantha macromeris

ee page 351 for
larger map

Size: H 2-9" (5-23 cm)

Shape: low-growing mounds, 8-40" (20-102 cm) wide, of 20-50 dome-shaped or short cylindrical stems

Stem: yellowish-to-grayish green stems, 1½-3¼" (4-8 cm) wide, covered with unusually large, flabby conical bumps (tubercles); each tubercle with short groove on top and tipped with white wool and spines; stem color is partly visible when plant is well hydrated

Spines: white, pale to dark gray, tan, brown or black; ⅝-2¾" (1.5-7 cm) long

Spine Clusters: straight flexible or tangled twisted spines in spine clusters; each cluster has 3-7 projecting dark central spines that are flattened and grooved on one side (lowest one points straight outward or curves downward), and 9-15 shorter paler radial spines

Flower: rosy pink or magenta flowers atop stem; each bloom, 1½-3" (4-7.5 cm) wide, has long narrow petals with fringed tips, paler midsections and darker pink bases; yellow, white and purplish pink central flower parts

Blooming: May-September, but mainly June-August; 4-6 times a summer following good rains; opens midday, closes at night, does not reopen the next day

Fruit: pear-shaped green pod, ⁷⁄₁₀" (1.8 cm) long, turns dark green or tan with the dried flower tuft remaining attached; sweetly fragrant, pinkish white pulp contains reddish brown seeds

southern Texas variety

shorter tubercle groove

tangled, twisted spines

Habitat: desert scrub and thorn scrub from 100-4,000' (30-1,220 m); open areas or under bushes; sandy, gravelly, or clay soils derived from a wide variety of rock types

Range: far western Texas and a smaller area extending east of the Pecos River; also in the extreme southern part of the state

**Big-needle Beehive
Cactus**
low-growing mounds of
many stems

**Whiskerbush Beehive
Cactus** *(pg. 83)*
single-stemmed or
a few stems

Longmamma Pincushion
(pg. 59)
shorter spines,
yellow flower

Compare: The similar Whiskerbush Beehive Cactus (pg. 83) grows as a single stem or a few stems, not in mounds like Big-needle Beehive Cactus. Longmamma Pincushion (pg. 59) mounds superficially resemble the rounded mats of Big-needle Beehive, but Longmamma has much shorter spines and yellow blooms.

Notes: This cactus forms low-growing mounds of abundant stems with untidy spine clusters. Species name *macromeris* means "large parts" in Greek, referring to the remarkable large, flabby bumps (tubercles). Big-needle Beehive has tubercle grooves that are short, a length unique among beehive cacti. The groove runs only a quarter to three-quarters the length of each tubercle on the upper side, from the tip toward the base. In other members of the genus *Coryphantha*, this groove runs the entire length of the tubercle.

A separate population found in extreme southern Texas near the Rio Grande is a variety of Big-needle, looking somewhat different with fewer spines and tubercles of widely varying sizes. This variety has even more stems than the far western Texas form, with immature stems often concealing the mature stems. Some of its tubercles lack spines altogether. Immature plants of Big-needle also are variable, often having only 5-7 radial spines and lacking central spines.

Unlike most cacti, Big-needle has no particular soil preference, thus it is common throughout its range in Texas. Also found in southern New Mexico and northern Mexico.

spines

flower

fruit

Sneed Beehive Cactus

Coryphantha sneedii

see page 351 for
larger map

Size: H 1-10½" (2.5-27 cm)

Shape: variable clumps of up to 250 upright rigid stems; many of the stems are immature

Stem: few to many, round or cylindrical, flat-topped stems appearing overall snowy white; each stem, ⅝-3" (1.5-7.5 cm) wide, with dense spines obscuring the green stem color

Spines: mostly snowy white, but also tan, yellow, pale pink, purplish gray or pinkish brown; fading to gray with age; ⅜-1" (.9-2.5 cm) long; larger spines sometimes with dark tips

Spine Clusters: 34-74 fine needle-like spines per cluster; each cluster has 9-22 central spines pointing out or pressed against the stem (inner central spines arranged like wagon wheel spokes around center of cluster) and 25-52 radial spines pressed closely against the stem

Flower: several pink flowers on flat tops of stems; each bloom, 1" (2.5 cm) wide, outer petals with fringed cream-colored edges and reddish brown midstripes, inner pale pink petals with dark pink midstripes; pink and orangish yellow male flower parts (stamens) and a white female flower part (stigma)

Blooming: March-June, may bloom again after summer rains; opens midday, closes before dusk, lasts 2-3 days

Fruit: slim egg-shaped pod, ⅔" (1.6 cm) long, turns yellowish green or bright red; flower tuft remains attached; contains reddish brown seeds; ripens 2 months after blooming

Habitat: desert scrub and pine woodlands from 2,000-8,700' (610-2,650 m); limestone outcrops, rocky hillsides

Range: scattered areas in far western Texas

Sneed Beehive Cactus
overall smaller, with central spines radiating out from center of cluster

Common Beehive Cactus
(pg. 123)
less spines in cluster, central spines resemble bird's foot

Cob Beehive Cactus
(pg. 127)
overall larger; central spines resemble bird's foot

Compare: The overall larger and closely related Common Beehive Cactus (pg. 123) is often mistaken for Sneed Beehive Cactus, but Common has fewer spines per cluster than Sneed with an arrangement of central spines like a bird's foot, rather than the wagon wheel-like, radiating central spines of Sneed. This difference in central spines can be difficult to discern. Cob Beehive Cactus (pg. 127) and Sneed are similar, but Cob often has darker-colored spines, as well as the hard-to-see bird's foot arrangement of the upper central spines.

Notes: Sneed Beehive Cactus is a variable, small cactus with nine different-looking varieties. Widespread and most commonly seen, the variety found in Big Bend National Park has slim cylindrical white stems and occurs at lower elevations in the hottest conditions. This Big Bend variety grows as a single stem or (as an older plant) in clumps of 5-25 stems. Other varieties are seen less often since they occur high on rock outcrops in steep mountains. A many-branching variety with round stems is found in the Franklin Mountains, near El Paso. Sneed is also found in extreme southeastern Arizona, in southern New Mexico and northern Mexico.

Two endangered varieties have become favorites among cactus enthusiasts who propagate the plants from seed or stems. These varieties form dome-shaped mounds of small round stems when cultivated in pots, and many flowers open simultaneously on the flat tops of the stems. Cold hardy to -13°F (-25°C) and unusually tolerant of wet conditions in cultivation.

spines

flower

fruit

CYLINDRICAL

Fishhook

Short-hook Fishhook Cactus
Ancistrocactus brevihamatus

see page 351 for
larger map

Size: H 1¾-5" (4.5-13 cm); W 1¾-3½" (4.5-9 cm)

Shape: egg-shaped cactus with only the larger end showing above ground

Stem: single green stem with 8-13 rows of prominent bumps (tubercles); each tubercle tipped with spine clusters that partially or completely cover the stem color

Spines: gray or white; yellowish brown, rust or tan; tips are yellow-brown to reddish brown; ⅔-2¾" (1.6-7 cm) long

Spine Clusters: formidable-looking spine clusters; each cluster has 4 flattened central spines (3 pointing up and curved against the stem; 1 largest central spine points out and is tipped with a short hook) surrounded by 7-14 slimmer shorter radial spines curving back against the stem

Flower: greenish yellow, pinkish brown or brownish green blossoms only partially open at the top of stem; each flower, ¾-1¼" (2-3 cm) wide, has orangish yellow male flower parts (stamens) and a pale green female flower part (stigma); flowers have a darker-colored stripe on each petal

Blooming: January-March; closes at night, lasts up to 9 days

Fruit: oval green pod, ½-1" (1-2.5 cm) long, stays green or turns slightly pinkish green when ripe; fruit walls dry to tan and become papery thin, but do not split open; contains shiny reddish brown seeds

CYLINDRICAL STEMS; **Fishhook 147**

Habitat: desert scrub, thorn scrub, sparse grasslands and oak/juniper woodlands from 1,000-4,100' (305-1,250 m); flats, hills, among creosote bushes; limestone or gypsum rocky soils

Range: Big Bend area of far western Texas and an area east of the Pecos River

Short-hook Fishhook Cactus
1 hooked central spine, fewer radial spines lack hooks

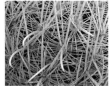

Scheer Fishhook Cactus
(pg. 151)
shaggier, with many more radial spines

Chihuahuan Fishhook Cactus *(pg. 155)*
some hooked radial spines

Compare: Short-hook Fishhook Cactus looks a lot like the closely related Scheer Fishhook Cactus (pg. 151). Scheer has more radial spines, so it appears shaggier than Short-hook. The very similar Chihuahuan Fishhook Cactus (pg. 155) has hooked radial as well as central spines, whereas only one central spine per cluster is hooked in Short-hook.

Notes: A small, single-stemmed cactus that can appear shaggy due to the varying lengths of the spines. The spine cluster at the tip of each bump (tubercle) has a stout hooked central spine, giving rise to "Fishhook" in the common name. Younger plants lack the hooked central spine and have scattered prominent tubercles, which in older plants are arranged in rows.

Short-hook Fishhook Cactus is a member of the genus *Ancistrocactus*. This genus name is derived from the Greek word for "fishhook." Closely related to other fishhook cacti such as Chihuahuan Fishhook Cactus. Fishhook cacti were once classified as members of a larger genus called *Sclerocactus*. These interesting cacti are popularly cultivated in Europe, where cactus aficionados grow them from seed indoors in pots.

spines

flower

fruit

CYLINDRICAL

Fishhook

Scheer Fishhook Cactus
Ancistrocactus scheeri

see page 351 for
larger map

Size: H 1¾-7" (4.5-18 cm); W 1¾-3¼" (4.5-8 cm)

Shape: round or cylindrical cactus, or club-shaped atop a stalk; branching in old age

Stem: single (sometimes multiple) green stem, with 8-13 rows of prominent rounded bumps (tubercles) tipped with spine clusters that completely cover the stem color

Spines: translucent yellowish brown, or tan to white, with reddish brown-to-dark brown tips; spines turn whitish gray with age; ¼-2" (.6-5 cm) long

Spine Clusters: tangle of formidable-looking spine clusters; each cluster has 3-4 flattened or compressed central spines (3 pointing straight upward, the lowest largest central spine points outward and is hooked) surrounded by 13-28 thinner radial spines pressed against the stem

Flower: greenish yellow or bright green blossoms at the top of stem; each flower, ¾-1¼" (2-3 cm) wide, has a darker-colored stripe on the outer petals, orangish yellow male flower parts (stamens) and a pale green female flower part (stigma); blossoms are held partly closed by the spines and never fully open

Blooming: November-March

Fruit: oblong green pod, 1-1½" (2.5-4 cm) long, turning powdery orange when ripe; fruit walls dry to tan and become papery thin, but do not split open; contains shiny, reddish brown seeds

Habitat: thorn scrub from 65-1,000' (20-305 m); flats, low hills; sandy, silty or loamy soils

Range: southern Texas

Scheer Fishhook Cactus
flowers held partially
closed by spines

Twisted-rib Cactus
(pg. 159)
tubercles compressed
vertically into thin ridges

Twisted-rib Cactus
(pg. 159)
yellow and red flower
opens fully

Compare: Twisted-rib Cactus (pg. 159) can look like Scheer Fishhook Cactus, especially when immature. Differs from Sheer Fishhook by its bumps (tubercles) compressed vertically into thin ridges on ribs that twist around the stem. Twisted-rib stem color shows through its fewer, horizontal, bright white radial spines. Twisted-rib flowers open fully and are not held partially closed by spines as they are in Scheer.

Notes: A very shaggy, usually single-stemmed cactus that looks much like a small haystack or a tuft of dead grass. Scheer has a stem that is constricted at the base, providing a delicate connection to the fleshy, tuberous roots.

Called a fishhook cactus for the one prominent hooked central spine below the other three straight, upward-pointing central spines in each cluster. A young Scheer has a narrowly cylindrical stem and lacks the hooked central spine, but has numerous short radial spines arranged like the teeth of a comb and tightly pressed against the stem. The stem broadens with age, and the new spines on the older stem are longer, coarser and more loosely held.

Interestingly, nectar glands are found in a small groove at the top of each tubercle, with a new gland growing and becoming active each year. These glands secrete high-sucrose nectar, upon which ants feed. The ants may provide benefits to the cactus in return by protecting the stem from chewing insects or by distributing the seeds.

spines

flower

fruit

CYLINDRICAL

Fishhook

Chihuahuan Fishhook Cactus
Glandulicactus uncinatus

e page 351 for
larger map

Size: H 3-6" (7.5-15 cm); W 2-3" (5-7.5 cm)

Shape: round, oval, or short cylindrical cactus; sometimes branching at the base

Stem: single bluish or grayish green stem with 9-13 deeply notched, well-defined ribs made up of nearly separated, compressed bumps (tubercles); each tubercle topped with a wool-filled groove; ribs are lined with spine clusters that do not obscure the stem color

Spines: straw-colored to pale gray; some pinkish yellow or reddish tan; ¾-5" (2-13 cm) long

Spine Clusters: mixture of straight, curved and hooked spines in clusters; each cluster has 1-4 central spines (main central spine is dull yellow, points upward and has a prominent hook) and 5-8 slightly flattened (3 lower are hooked) radial spines pressed against the stem

Flower: deep rusty red or orange blossoms at the top of stem; each cylindrical flower, ¾-1¼" (2-3 cm) wide, has paler petal edges, russet and yellow male flower parts (stamens) and a pale red female flower part (stigma)

Blooming: March-May, rarely in late summer; opens mid-morning, partially closes at night, lasts 2-3 days

Fruit: oval fleshy green pod, ⅝-1" (1.5-2.5 cm) long, with many conspicuous fringed white scales; turns bright red when ripe, but does not split open; mealy pulp is white and contains black seeds; ripens May-June

Habitat: desert scrub and grasslands from 300-5,000' (90-1,525 m); flats, hills, among clumps of grass; volcanic or limestone soils

Range: far western Texas and an isolated area in the southern part of the state

Chihuahuan Fishhook Cactus
looks like a clump of dead grass

Turk's Head Barrel
(pg. 231)
looks like a tiny haystack

Glory-of-Texas *(pg. 171)*
also can resemble a tiny haystack

Compare: An immature Turk's Head Barrel (pg. 231) can look like Chihuahuan Fishhook Cactus–both of which resemble tiny haystacks or clumps of dead grass. Turk's Head differs from Chihuahuan Fishhook by lacking hooked radial spines. Even in immature Chihuahuan Fishhook plants, most of the radial spines are curved or hooked. Glory-of-Texas (pg. 171) also has long spines like Chihuahuan Fishhook, but its ribbon-like radial spines are flattened and twisted, not hooked.

Notes: Of more than 80 cactus species in the state, most occur in the region west of the Pecos River in far western Texas, often not far from the Mexico border. Texas has more cacti than any other state, but many are small and inconspicuous, unlike the large, obvious cacti in Arizona. Chihuahuan Fishhook is found only in Texas and New Mexico in the United States, but is widespread in Mexico.

Genus name *Glandulicactus* is for the dome-shaped nectar glands in woolly grooves atop the bumps (tubercles). Species name *uncinatus* is from the Latin word for "hook," referring to the hooked central and radial spines. Extending well past the top of the stem, the long central spines appear too large for this small cactus. Sometimes called Cat's Claw Cactus. Closely related to and once a member of the genus *Hamatocactus* due to the similar fruit and hooked central spines of cacti in that genus. Looks much like Short-hook Fishhook Cactus (pg. 147), although Short-hook is in the *Ancistrocactus* genus.

spines

flower

immature fruit

see page 352 for larger map

Twisted-rib Cactus

Hamatocactus bicolor

Size: H 1⅜-8" (3.5-20 cm)

Shape: round or cylindrical stem, or branching at the base into clumps of different-sized stems

Stem: single or multiple green stems; each stem has 13 spiraling or vertical ribs of compressed bumps (tubercles) fused to form a slender ridge; each tubercle has a felted groove, 1-2 peg-shaped golden nectar glands at the top and is tipped with a spine cluster; spine clusters do not cover the stem color

Spines: white, tan or yellowish brown; becoming ashy gray or reddish brown; ½-1½" (1-4 cm) long

Spine Clusters: flexible needle-like spine clusters; each cluster has 1 long hooked central spine pointing outward surrounded by 10-19 thinner white radial spines that look like white bow ties from a distance

Flower: yellow and red blooms at the top of stem; each flower, 1½-3" (4-7.5 cm) wide, has inner petals with red bases; outer petals are green with reddish brown edges; red and yellow male flower parts (stamens); a pale yellow-to-orange female flower part (stigma)

Blooming: April-October; opening midmorning, closing at night, only open 1 day

Fruit: round, fleshy, dark green pod, ½" (1 cm) wide, with a dried floral tuft and a few fringed white scales; turns scarlet red when ripe in late fall; releases black seeds through a vertical slit

southern Texas form

2 nectar glands and red fruit

Habitat: grasslands, thorn scrub and woodlands up to 1,000' (305 m); mesquite thickets, flats, low hills, limestone soils

Range: central and southern Texas

Twisted-rib Cactus
indistinct tubercles
compressed vertically
into thin-ridged ribs

Turk's Head Barrel
(pg. 231)
ribs show more
prominent tubercles

Turk's Head Barrel
(pg. 231)
yellow flower with
yellow center

Compare: Small plants of Turk's Head Barrel (pg. 231) can look much like Twisted-rib Cactus. The slender ribs of Turk's Head show more prominent bumps (tubercles) and longer central spines than those of Twisted-rib. Turk's Head has larger yellow flowers, not flowers with red bases on inner petals like those of Twisted-rib.

Notes: The only species in this genus, which is closely related to other fishhook cacti in the *Ancistrocactus*, *Glandulicactus*, *Thelocactus* and *Ferocactus* genera. The genus name *Hamatocactus*, derived from Latin and Greek words, means "hooked spine." Species name *bicolor* refers to the yellow and red flowers. "Twisted-rib" is for the slender, ridged ribs that spiral around the stem as the cactus ages.

This species has two distinct forms. The typical form has wide, round, dark green stems with slender ribs and few spines that do not obscure the color of the stems. The form found in southern Texas has more spines, and mature plants have conical or cylindrical stems with spines that give the plants a yellowish tan appearance. Both forms have single hooked central spines, and white and tan radial spines that look like bright white bow ties sprinkled on the stems. The single central spines of immature plants are also hooked.

Blooms in spring to fall. Flowers arise from the wool-filled groove next to the spine clusters on top of the upper tubercles. This groove also holds two golden nectar glands and the round fruit. A cold-hardy cactus, Twisted-rib is easy to grow outdoors in well-drained soils.

161

spines

flower

fruit

ee page 352 for
larger map

CYLINDRICAL

Fishhook

Horse Crippler

Echinocactus texensis

Size: H 4-8" (10-20 cm); W 4-12" (10-30 cm)

Shape: flat-topped round cactus or dome-shaped with stem only partly above ground; shrinks to below ground level in drought

Stem: pale grayish green or deep green stem topped with short dense cream-colored wool; stem is rock hard and has 13-27 narrow vertical ribs lined with claw-like spine clusters

Spines: gray, pale tan or pink to red; 1½-3" (4-7.5 cm) long

Spine Clusters: widely spaced clusters do not overlap; each cluster has 1 central spine curving downward or pointing straight outward and 6-7 spreading radial spines; slightly fuzzy, flattened spines have horizontal ridges

Flower: cup-shaped, silvery or rosy pink flowers at the top of stem; each upright blossom, 2-2½" (5-6 cm) wide, has fringed petals with red or orange bases, red and yellow male flower parts (stamens) and a pale pink female flower part (stigma)

Blooming: April-May; opening late morning, closing at night, lasting 1-3 days

Fruit: round fleshy green pod, ⅝-2" (1.5-5 cm) long, partially covered with white wool and topped with a dried floral tuft; turns bright red when ripe and loses its wool, revealing tiny barbs in triangular white areas (areoles) on the fruit wall; contains black seeds

Habitat: desert scrub, thorn scrub, grasslands and oak shrublands up to 5,500' (1,675 m); flats, lower slopes, saline flats; deep limestone, volcanic, or water-deposited soils

Range: west central and southern Texas, and an area west of the Pecos River

Horse Crippler
longer spines, stems
never cylindrical

Eagle's Claw Cactus
(pg. 167)
shorter spines, stems can
be cylindrical in old age

Fishhook Barrel (pg. 235)
bristle-like radial spines

Compare: The closely related Eagle's Claw Cactus (pg. 167) is the cactus most likely to be mistaken for Horse Crippler. Eagle's Claw has shorter spines, and its stems grow taller and cylindrical with age, while Horse Crippler has longer spines and remains dome-shaped. Horse Crippler cacti look similar to the small plants of Fishhook Barrel (pg. 235), but have stout radial spines, quite unlike the bristle-like white radial spines of Fishhook Barrels.

Notes: Low growing and often concealed by grasses, Horse Crippler is named for the outward-pointing central spine that is sharp and tough enough to puncture a horse's hoof or a car tire. Also called Devil's Claw. The part of Horse Crippler protruding above ground resembles the top part of a barrel cactus, but Horse Crippler remains flat-topped or dome-shaped and never attains the height and barrel shape of a barrel cactus. More widespread in Texas than most cactus species in the state. Also occurs in southeastern New Mexico and the Mexican states of Coahuila, Durango, Nuevo León and Tamaulipas.

Cold hardy to 0°F (-18°C) or lower, tolerant of more moisture than other cacti and adapts to a wide range of habitats. Interest in growing hardy cacti has exploded with increased availability of inexpensive nursery plants propagated from seed and has resulted in more numerous skilled and adventurous gardeners. There are now cactus enthusiasts in New England, the upper Midwest and the Pacific Northwest who grow a large number of cactus species outdoors.

spines

fruit

CYLINDRICAL

Fishhook

Eagle's Claw Cactus
Echinocactus horizonthalonius

see page 352 for
larger map

Size: H 2-12" (5-30 cm); W 3-6" (7.5-15 cm)

Shape: dome-shaped or short cylindrical stem; sometimes flat-topped

Stem: single dark bluish gray or yellowish green stem topped with dense cream-colored wool; stem has 7-9 (usually 8) broad ribs lined with stout spine clusters; ribs are vertical or spiralling around the stem

Spines: gray, pink, tan or dark brown spines; $^7/_{10}$-1$^1/_2$" (1.8-4 cm) long

Spine Clusters: widely spaced clusters do not overlap; each cluster has 5-10 (usually 8) similar radial and central spines that are curved or straight; 3 lower central spines curve downward, resembling the claws on an eagle's foot; spines have horizontal ridges

Flower: cup-shaped, bright pink flowers at the top of stem; each upright blossom, 2" (5 cm) wide, has fringed petals with dark pink bases surrounding bright yellow male flower parts (stamens) and a pink or olive female flower part (stigma)

Blooming: April-July, but mainly May or early June; opening midday, closing at night

Fruit: smooth oval pod, $^1/_2$-1" (1-2.5 cm) long, mostly covered with cream-colored wool and topped with a dried floral tuft; turns pink when ripe, then quickly dries to papery tan, sometimes splitting open or sometimes releasing black seeds through a pore in the base

Habitat: desert scrub, grasslands and mountains from 2,500-5,500' (760-1,675 m); flats, dry rocky slopes; ledges of limestone and volcanic rock or in clay or gypsum soils

Range: far western Texas

Eagle's Claw Cactus
8 broad ribs, curved
central spines

Horse Crippler *(pg. 163)*
13-27 narrow ribs

Fishhook Barrel *(pg. 235)*
hooked central spine,
bristle-like radial spines

Compare: With its stout formidable spines, the related Horse Crippler (pg. 163) looks similar to Eagle's Claw Cactus, but its many ridged narrow ribs outnumber the eight broad ribs of Eagle's Claw. The stem of Eagle's Claw is also similar in shape to an immature Fishhook Barrel (pg. 235) stem, but Fishhook Barrel has bristle-like radial spines and a hooked central spine. Eagle's Claw radial spines are stout like its central spines, which are curved, not hooked.

Notes: Can grow from dome-shaped, becoming a short cylindrical or barrel-shaped cactus, especially in Big Bend National Park in far western Texas, where large older plants are found. Also called Blue Barrel since it can look much like a small barrel cactus. In the rest of the state, it is more likely to remain the size and shape of half of a grapefruit. Eagle's Claw is the smallest of the three U.S. species in the genus *Echinocactus,* and all have lots of wool at the center of the flattened stem top. Eagle's Claw bright pink flowers and woolly fruit spring from underneath this wool. Desert birds use the wool to line their nests.

Flowers mainly in May or early June, with most of the plants in a population blooming simultaneously. Sometimes flowers again 3-12 days after summer rains, up to three times a year. Bees pollinate the blossoms, and pack rats and birds eat the resulting fruit and seeds. Eagle's Claw grows well in a container.

spines

flower

immature fruit

Glory-of-Texas
Thelocactus bicolor

e page 352 for
larger map

Size: H 2-15" (5-38 cm); W 1½-4" (4-10 cm)

Shape: round or conical cactus; sometimes branching at the base into clumps of similar-sized stems

Stem: single or multiple, grayish or yellowish green stems; stem has 8-13 spiraling rows of crowded prominent broad bumps (tubercles) fused at their bases; each tubercle tipped with spine clusters that partially or completely cover the stem color

Spines: bicolored (straw-colored, gray or white at base and tips, red middle section) spines, aging to gray; ½-2½" (1-6 cm) long

Spine Clusters: neat or tangled spine clusters; each cluster has 1-4 central spines (1 flattened, straight, red or gray central spine pointing out or down; others similar to radials); 12-20 white or yellow radial spines (upper are ribbon-like, flattened and twisted; lower are needle-like and pressed against the stem)

Flower: magenta blooms in tuft at top of stem; each flower, 1½-3" (4-7.5 cm) wide, has satiny inner petals with a white band above the red bases; paler outer petals; red and yellow male flower parts (stamens); a white and salmon-colored female flower part (stigma)

Blooming: February-May, sometimes July-September; 7-10 days after heavy rains; opening about noon, closing at night

Fruit: rounded fleshy green pod, ½" (1 cm) long, with a dried floral tuft and many fringed scales; turns brownish red and dries rapidly after ripening; releases black seeds through a pore at the base

yellow-spined form

Habitat: desert scrub, grasslands and thorn scrub from 200-4,500' (60-1,370 m); flats, hills, basins, bajadas; gravelly volcanic or silty, water-deposited soils

Range: Big Bend region in far western Texas and a small area in the far southern part of the state

Glory-of-Texas
can resemble
Twisted-rib Cactus

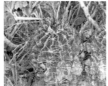

Twisted-rib Cactus
(pg. 159)
tubercles compressed and
fused into thin-ridged ribs

Twisted-rib Cactus
(pg. 159)
1 hooked central spine
per cluster

Compare: Glory-of-Texas is similar looking to Twisted-rib Cactus (pg. 159) when not in bloom. Bumps (tubercles) of both cacti form rows or fuse into ribs, which spiral around the stem. Twisted-rib has vertically compressed tubercles, each with a long hooked central spine, unlike the broad tubercles of Glory-of-Texas, which lack hooked spines.

Notes: Of the ten cactus species in the *Thelocactus* genus (all of which are found in Mexico), only one occurs in the United States. Common and widespread in the Chihuahuan Desert and Tamaulipan thorn scrub of northeastern Mexico, Glory-of-Texas crosses the border into the Big Bend region in far western Texas and into Starr County in far southern Texas. A smaller, yellow-spined variety is found solely in the Marathon Basin of Brewster County in far western Texas.

Although probably most closely related to Twisted-rib and other fishhook cacti, this plant lacks the hooked central spines of those species. Like fishhook cacti, however, the upper tubercles of Glory-of-Texas have a wide, wool-packed groove at the top that holds nectar glands. The blossoms also arise from this groove.

The green stems turn partially orangish red in severe drought, during which, together with the red middle sections of the spines, the entire cactus can appear red. Will tolerate cool days and nights. Fairly easy to cultivate and popular for its stunning, large pink flowers that can bloom indoors with sufficient light.

spines

flower

Davis Hedgehog
Echinocereus davisii

e page 352 for
larger map

Size: H ½-1¼" (1-3 cm); W ½-1" (1-2.5 cm)

Shape: single spiny round stem; rarely branching into 2-3 stems

Stem: small, upright, green-to-dark purple stem has 6-9 wavy vertical ribs made up of rows of joined bumps (tubercles) with spines that partly hide the stem color

Spines: gray or white with black, dark reddish brown or dark purplish brown tips; ⅝" (1.5 cm) long

Spine Clusters: closely spaced clusters; each has 8-15 sturdy radial spines that are straight in younger plants and curving outward in all directions in older plants

Flower: several small greenish yellow flowers along the sides at midstem; each flower, 1" (2.5 cm) wide, is on a spiny stalk and has slender petals with maroon midstripes around pale yellow and green flower parts

Blooming: February-March

Fruit: spiny oval pod, ½" (1 cm) long, remains green or turns purplish brown when ripe; has white pulp containing many small seeds; fruit ripens 2 months after flowering

Habitat: semideserts and grasslands between 3,900-4,400' (1,190-1,340 m); rock outcrops, hidden below mats of spike moss, under rocks or shrubs

Range: limited to Marathon Basin in the Chihuahuan Desert in Brewster County in far western Texas

Davis Hedgehog
longer spines on tubercles
arranged in rows

**Green-flowered
Hedgehog** *(pg. 203)*
relatively shorter spines

**Whiskerbush Beehive
Cactus** *(pg. 83)*
tubercles not arranged
in rows

Compare: Davis Hedgehog may be mistaken for a seedling of many hedgehog species, but is easily identified as a mature tiny plant when flowering or fruiting. Related to Green-flowered Hedgehog (pg. 203), but Davis has longer spines than any variety of Green-flowered occurring in the same area. Whiskerbush Beehive Cactus (pg. 83) can appear similar to Davis, but the obvious bumps (tubercles) of Whiskerbush Beehive are not arranged in rows like those of Davis.

Notes: This is one of the smallest cacti in the world. Also known as Dwarf Hedgehog. Grows buried in soil, with less than 1 inch (2.5 cm) of the stem showing above the ground. Usually also protected from wind and sun exposure under mats of Resurrection Plant, a spike moss that can survive almost complete water loss.

State and federally listed as an endangered species. Occurs only in far western Texas within a basin 30-40 miles (48-64 km) wide, in rocky soil composed of very hard, dense, quartz-like rock (novaculite). Since prehistoric times, novaculite has been used to make arrow and spear points and as sharpening stones.

Once a variety of Green-flowered, but Davis is now considered a separate species because it blooms earlier in the spring. Davis is still thought to be closely related to Green-flowered since their flowers look alike and arise from the same location (the sides of stems).

spines

flower

immature fruit

CYLINDRICAL

Hedgehog

ee page 352 for
larger map

Lace Hedgehog
Echinocereus reichenbachii

Size: H 3-6" (7.5-15 cm)

Shape: single short cylindrical stem or branching into 2-12 stems; immature plants are round

Stem: dark green stem, 1-3" (2.5-7.5 cm) wide, with 10-19 slightly wavy vertical ribs that are obscured by interlacing spines during drought; sometimes spines form subtle horizontal bands of alternating colors

Spines: white or brown with dull pink, dark brown or reddish black tips; $^1/_{10}$-1" (.2-2.5 cm) long

Spine Clusters: many-spined, overlapping clusters; each cluster lacks central spines (rarely has 1-2 very short central spines) and has 12-36 stiff radial spines, spreading and arranged in comb-like fashion on each side of a long oval raised area (areole); areoles near top of stem have white wool

Flower: pink or magenta flowers on woolly, fine-spined stalks just below stem tip; each cup-shaped bloom, 2-4" (5-10 cm) wide, has overlapping petals (inner petals have red, green or white bases) around a pale yellow center

Blooming: April-May

Fruit: elongated, elliptical, dark green pod, 2½" (6 cm) long, covered with woolly white hairs and fine dark brown spines that drop off when fruit is ripe; fleshy white pulp contains many small black seeds

CYLINDRICAL STEMS; **Hedgehog 179**

round-stemmed
young plant

flame-shaped
flower

Habitat: desert scrub, grasslands, thorn scrub and oak/juniper woodlands from 100-4,000' (30-1,220 m); limestone rock outcrops, among grasses or under bushes; limestone or other sandy soils

Range: northwestern, central and southern Texas

Lace Hedgehog
flower stalk is white and
woolly with fine dark
brown spines

**Mexican Rainbow
Hedgehog** (pg. 191)
flower stalk and fruit
have separated white
spine clusters

**Mexican Rainbow
Hedgehog** (pg. 191)
has central spines

Compare: When not flowering or in fruit, Lace Hedgehog can be mistaken for Mexican Rainbow Hedgehog (pg. 191), as both have comb-like radial spines and white wool in the upper circular areas (areoles). The flower stalks and immature fruit of Lace are totally covered in woolly white hairs and fine dark spines, while Mexican Rainbow have distinct white spine clusters. Stem spine clusters of Lace usually lack central spines; Mexican Rainbow has 2-3 central spines.

Notes: Although found mainly in Texas, Lace Hedgehog also grows in Colorado, Oklahoma, New Mexico and Mexico. Lace Hedgehogs occurring in Texas usually do not have central spines. The many stiff radial spines look like twin combs on each side of the slim areoles.

During drought when the cactus shrinks in size, the radial spines overlap, interlocking with other clusters and obscuring the stem color. After rains, the well-hydrated plant expands, revealing the dark green-to-dark purplish green stem between the rows of spines. Lacking leaves, green chlorophyll in the stem skin cells use the sun's energy to make food (photosynthesis).

Also called Purple Candle or Black Lace Cactus for the purplish pink, flame-shaped flowers atop the dark stems of one variety. This variety of Lace Hedgehog is listed as endangered by the Center for Plant Conservation, a network of botanical institutions dedicated to saving native plants.

spines

flower

Allicoche Hedgehog
Echinocereus papillosus

ee page 353 for
larger map

Size: H 1½-8" (4-20 cm)

Shape: irregular clumps of 2-95 stems branching from the base; older stems on outside of clumps lean or sprawl on the ground

Stem: upright, cylindrical, deep or pale green stems; each stem, 1-3" (2.5-7.5 cm) wide, has 7-10 distinctly wavy ribs divided into conspicuous bumps (tubercles) not covered up by the spines

Spines: white, yellowish brown, or brown and white; ⅝-1" (1.5-2.5 cm) long

Spine Clusters: each cluster has 1 (can have up to 4) straight brown and yellow central spine pointing straight outward or downward and 7-10 straight radial spines spreading or pressed against the stem

Flower: 2-3 pale yellow and red flowers atop spiny bulbous stalks at the tops of stems; each funnel-shaped flower, 2½-4" (6-10 cm) wide, has an orangish red throat, pale yellow male flower parts (stamens) and a green female flower part (stigma)

Blooming: February-early March

Fruit: rounded green pod, ¾" (2 cm) long, covered with short bristles, remains green when ripe and contains white pulp; fruit ripens about 2 months after flowering

Habitat: prairies with scattered mesquite trees, plains near the Rio Grande and thorn scrub up to 500' (150 m); mesquite thickets; red or limestone gravelly soils

Range: southern Texas

Allicoche Hedgehog
spine cluster has 1 central
spine pointing straight out
or down

Pitaya *(pg. 215)*
flabby stems, sparse spines
resemble Allicoche

**Sea Urchin Beehive
Cactus** *(pg. 111)*
similar flower has
reddish orange, not
yellow, stamens

Compare: With its flabby sprawling stems and sparse spines, a small Pitaya (pg. 215) might be mistaken for Allicoche Hedgehog. However, Pitaya has pink, not yellow, flowers and thicker stems. The unrelated Sea Urchin Beehive Cactus (pg. 111) has flowers that look somewhat like Allicoche flowers. The orange throats of Sea Urchin blooms come from the reddish orange male flower parts (stamens) instead of the red on the bases of the inner layer of petals in Allicoche flowers.

Notes: This small clumping cactus has short stems dotted with long central spines arising from the prominent bumps (tubercles) in the ribs. The species name *papillosus* means "soft protuberances," referring to the tubercles.

Originates from the southern tip of Texas. Although still found there in the wild, it is seen by few people since it occurs only on private land. Allicoche also grows in Mexico.

Widely cultivated by cactus enthusiasts. The red-throated, pale yellow flowers are enormous relative to the size of the stems. Blooming in early spring, this is a wonderful container plant, but does not do well when planted outside anywhere north of southern Texas. Available from nurseries in the United States and Europe as seed, small plants or 4-year-old plants nearly ready to bloom. Sometimes sold under the names Yellow Allicoche or Miniature Hedgehog.

spines

flower

fruit

CYLINDRICAL

Hedgehog

Fendler Hedgehog

Echinocereus fendleri

See page 353 for larger map

Size: H 3-7" (7.5-18 cm)

Shape: loose clusters of 1-10 cylindrical stems

Stem: multiple upright or reclining, semisoft stems, each 1½-3" (4-7.5 cm) wide, dark green with 8-11 wavy rows of large bumps (tubercles) with sparse spines

Spines: black or brown or white to gray with a dark stripe beneath; ½-1½" (1-4 cm) long

Spine Clusters: clusters line each row; each cluster has 1 (sometimes 2-3) longer, dark-tipped, outward-pointing central spine that sometimes curves upward, surrounded by 4-10 short stout radial spines pressed against the stem, with the longest radial spine pointing downward

Flower: 1 to several funnel-shaped, brilliant magenta blooms on the sides of stems near the top; each large flower, 2-4½" (5-11 cm) wide, has layers of petals with darker bases and midstripes and a center of pale yellow and green

Blooming: mid-April through mid-May

Fruit: spiny oval red pod, ¾-1¼" (2-3 cm) long, drops most of its white spines when ripe, with magenta-to-red pulp containing many small black seeds

Habitat: deserts, plains and grasslands from 3,500-5,500' (1,065-1,675 m); mountain basins and slopes, bajadas, ridges; limestone or volcanic rocky soils

Range: far western Texas

Fendler Hedgehog
dark brown stripe on
radial spines

Scarlet Hedgehog
(pg. 211)
radial and central spines
look alike

Scarlet Hedgehog
(pg. 211)
orangish red flowers

Compare: Somewhat resembles Scarlet Hedgehog (pg. 211), but Scarlet has larger stems and all similar-looking spines. Unlike Fendler Hedgehog, Scarlet radial spines do not have a dark brown stripe beneath. Scarlet also differs from Fendler by its orangish red, not pink, flowers.

Notes: Seventeen species of hedgehog cacti occur in Texas, more than in any other state. The Chihuahuan Desert, which covers more area in Texas than in Arizona or New Mexico, is renowned for having the largest variety of cactus species of any of the four deserts in North America.

Although limited in Texas to the far western desert and plains, grasslands and mountain basins, this wide-ranging cactus is also found in Arizona, southeastern Colorado, most of New Mexico and northern Mexico. Growing at higher elevations, the small Fendler has fewer spines and is shorter than most hedgehogs in Texas. Immature woolly plants (with fewer and all-white spines) don't resemble mature plants. Fendler Hedgehog occurs in the wild as a solitary plant or in clumps of a few stems.

Frequently cultivated for its big, bright pink flowers, growing to maturity and blooming about five years after seeds are planted. After flowering in spring, the red pods ripen from June through August. The edible, sweet fruit does not stay on the cactus long since it is quickly eaten by birds and small mammals.

spines

flower

fruit

Mexican Rainbow Hedgehog

Echinocereus pectinatus

ee page 353 for
larger map

Size: H 3-8" (7.5-20 cm)

Shape: single, short, cylindrical or round stem; older plants branch near the base into 2-3 stout stems

Stem: smooth-looking stem, 2½-3" (6-7.5 cm) wide, with 14-18 slightly wavy vertical ribs lined with interlacing spines that mostly hide the green skin color; lacks the subtle horizontal bands of alternating colors found in other rainbow cacti

Spines: ashy white; largest spines with purplish brown tips; ⅙-½" (.4-1 cm) long

Spine Clusters: overlapping clusters; each cluster has 2-3 (can have up to 6) short central spines pointing outward and arranged in distinct vertical rows, and 15-24 longer radial spines pressed tightly against the stem; white wool present in upper spine clusters

Flower: pink flowers on spiny stalks grow just below stem tips; each vase-shaped bloom, 2-4" (5-10 cm) wide, has tricolored inner petals (pink with a middle band of white above a green base) around a yellow and green center

Blooming: March-May; opening in late morning, closing at night, lasting 2-3 days

Fruit: broadly oval, spiny green pod, 2½" (6 cm) long, turns a dull dark purplish red with juicy white pulp containing many small black seeds; ripens May-July

Habitat: desert scrub, thorn scrub and grasslands with a few juniper trees from 1,000-3,000' (305-915 m); limestone rock hillsides, mesas

Range: western Texas in areas along both sides of the southern portion of the Pecos River and northeast of the Rio Grande

Mexican Rainbow Hedgehog
inner petals have white bands and green bases

Texas Rainbow Hedgehog *(pg. 199)*
inner petals have yellow middle bands

Lace Hedgehog *(pg. 179)*
flower with a red throat

Compare: The closely related Texas Rainbow Hedgehog (pg. 199) has a short-spined form that can appear very much like Mexican Rainbow. Texas Rainbow sometimes has pink instead of yellow flowers, but the inner petals have yellow, not white, middle bands. The smaller Lace Hedgehog (pg. 179) has red-, green- or white-throated flowers, but lacks white middle bands and the tricolored effect of Mexican Rainbow blossoms.

Notes: A short, cylindrical or round, single-stemmed hedgehog with intensely pink or magenta flowers that have white bands and green bases. Mexican Rainbow is mostly found in north central Mexico, but ranges over the Rio Grande into Texas. Although commonly referred to as a rainbow hedgehog, the variety of Mexican Rainbow found in Texas does not the have horizontal contrasting color bands on its stems like most rainbow hedgehogs. However, plants in Mexico quite distinctly show pink and white bands on their stems.

Usually has 2-3 short, projecting central spines. Longer, rigid radial spines are pressed against the stem on each side of circular areas (areoles) in comb-like fashion, thus also called Comb Hedgehog.

Like other hedgehogs, its ribs store water, expanding like accordion pleats. In addition, the waxy skin, lack of leaves and shade from the white spines slow water loss due to evaporation. These features enable it to grow in the Chihuahuan Desert, where annual rainfall averages 6-12 inches (15-30 cm).

spines

flower

immature fruit

Hedgehog

See page 353 for larger map

Chisos Mountain Hedgehog

Echinocereus chisosensis

Size: H 5-8" (13-20 cm)

Shape: inconspicuous stem or small cluster of a few conical stems

Stem: upright or sagging green stems, branching with maturity; each stem, 1-2" (2.5-5 cm) wide, has 13-16 vertical wavy ribs with long spines that partially obscure the stem color, giving the plant a shaggy appearance

Spines: white, pinkish gray, pale pink, dark brown, or purplish black with brown tips; ⅓-3" (.8-7.5 cm) long

Spine Clusters: each cluster has 1-6 (usually 2) darker central spines pointing outward surrounded by 10-17 radial spines pressed against the stem, with longest radial lowest; puffy white wool in upper stem clusters

Flower: 1 to several funnel-shaped, rose pink flowers on long woolly spiny stalks on the sides of stems; each bloom, 2-3" (5-7.5 cm) wide, has petals with a pale band above the maroon base and pale yellow, maroon and dark green flower parts

Blooming: mid-March to mid-April; opening midmorning, partly closing at night, lasting 1-3 days

Fruit: oblong fleshy green pod, 1" (2.5 cm) long, spiny and covered with white wool, turns dull red when ripe and spines fall off, has dry white pulp containing many small black seeds

CYLINDRICAL

Habitat: desert scrub from 2,000-3,000' (610-915 m); ridges, bajadas, arroyos, under shrubs, among grasses or dog chollas; gravelly soils

Range: limited to only a small area in Big Bend National Park, southeast of the Chisos Mountains in far western Texas

Chisos Mountain Hedgehog
puffy balls of white wool in some areoles

Green-flowered Hedgehog *(pg. 203)*
less wool, but more spines

Green-flowered Hedgehog *(pg. 203)*
flower lacks long stalk

Compare: Most closely resembles the rusty-spined forms of Green-flowered Hedgehog (pg. 203), which also occur in Big Bend National Park. Rusty-spined forms of Green-flowered have smaller, rust-colored flowers. Green-flowered has much less white wool in its stem areoles and more spines in each cluster than does Chisos Mountain Hedgehog, and its flowers either lack or have smaller stalks than the long stalks of Chisos Mountain blooms.

Notes: The genus name *Echinocereus* comes from the Greek *echinos* for "hedgehog" or "spine" and *cereus* for "waxy," referring to the tough skin of the stems. Botanists continue to disagree about how to classify members of this confusing genus and how many species it includes. Currently, it is thought that there are about 15 hedgehog species in Texas, but there may 20 or more.

The rare and endangered Chisos Mountain Hedgehog is very limited in its range, occurring only in a small area of Big Bend National Park and nowhere else in the world. Of the 27 species of plants listed as threatened and endangered in Texas, ten are cacti. The numbers of Chisos Mountain Hedgehogs are declining, probably due to the drought of recent years. When stressed, the stems and spines turn dark purplish green and then gray, appearing dead. Blooms even during drought.

pink spines

white spines

immature fruit

Texas Rainbow Hedgehog
Echinocereus dasyacanthus

e page 353 for
larger map

Size: H 4½-9" (11-23 cm), sometimes up to 18" (45 cm)

Shape: single cylindrical stem or loose clumps of 2-20 stout stems branching from the base

Stem: rigid shaggy green stem, 2-3" (5-7.5 cm) wide, with 15-19 wavy vertical ribs obscured by interlacing spines; sometimes spines form subtle horizontal bands of alternating colors, indicating a year's growth

Spines: pink to pale yellow, white or tan (sometimes dark brown or purple); ⅕-¾" (.5-2 cm) long; with dark tips

Spine Clusters: many-spined, overlapping clusters in vertical rows that are sometimes difficult to distinguish; each cluster has 4-12 central spines pointing in all directions and 14-25 stiff radial spines pressed tightly against the stem

Flower: brilliant yellow or orange (less often red or pink) flowers on spiny stalks just below stem tips; each cup-shaped bloom, 3-4½" (7.5-11 cm) wide, has overlapping petals (inner petals often with green or different-colored bases); yellow and green center

Blooming: March-May; opening in the daytime, closing at night, lasting about 1 week

Fruit: rounded spiny green pod, 2½" (6 cm) long, ripens to a dull dark purplish red, containing juicy pink or white pulp with many small black seeds

Habitat: desert scrub and grasslands between 1,700-4,700' (520-1,435 m); valleys, rocky limestone hills, steep canyons

Range: far western Texas and an area in the west central part of the state

Texas Rainbow Hedgehog
large flowers grow near stem tips

Green-flowered Hedgehog *(pg. 203)*
smaller yellow flowers arise from side of stem

Green-flowered Hedgehog *(pg. 203)*
stems can have horizontal bands resembling Texas Rainbow bands

Compare: Green-flowered Hedgehog (pg. 203) has smaller flowers growing from the sides of stems well below the tip, while Texas Rainbow Hedgehog has large flowers close to the tops of stems. Short-spined forms of Green-flowered with horizontal bands could be mistaken for Texas Rainbow.

Notes: "Rainbow" in the common name refers to the contrasting colored bands on the stem, each reflecting a year's growth. Some populations have many white spines (thus lacking most of the pink color and horizontal bands) and appear overall white. Spines are usually numerous, overlapping and interlocking, forming a mesh that covers the green color of the stem. Also called Spiny Hedgehog. The species name *dasyacanthus* is Greek, meaning "shaggy spine."

Often seen growing on a rocky limestone hillside. When in bloom, this stout hedgehog is a pretty sight with its pink and white spines and conspicuous yellow flowers. The blooms appear in early March in lower elevations and later in the spring at higher elevations. The bee-pollinated blossoms are sweetly fragrant, attracting native wild bees and honeybees to the nectar and pollen. Ripening in June through August, the fruit is edible, but acidic.

Hybridizes readily with the red-flowered Scarlet Hedgehog (pg. 211) wherever they overlap in range, producing magenta flowers. Texas Rainbow Hedgehog is mostly found in Texas and New Mexico, but also occurs in northern Mexico.

spines

flower

fruit

see page 353 for larger map

Green-flowered Hedgehog
Echinocereus viridiflorus

Size: H 3-12" (7.5-30 cm)

Shape: single stem or small clumps of a few (rarely more than 12) round or short cylindrical stems

Stem: upright green stem, 1-3½" (2.5-9 cm) wide, with 10-20 prominent (sometimes wavy) ribs with spines that partially hide the stem color

Spines: variable; red and white, red and yellow, yellow and white, purplish brown or grayish white; ⅙-1½" (.4-4 cm) long; tips are often darker

Spine Clusters: closely spaced clusters of many straight or slightly curved spines; each cluster has up to 17 spreading or outward-pointing central spines with 12-38 shorter radial spines spreading or pressed close against the stem; sometimes lacks central spines

Flower: variable small flowers; green, yellow, peach, brown or rust, along the sides at midstem and atop a spiny stalk; each narrow, cup-shaped bloom, 1" (2 cm) wide, has petals with darker maroon midstripes around fuzzy green and yellow flower parts

Blooming: March-June

Fruit: spiny oval pod, ½" (1 cm) long, is dark green, yellowish or reddish green, or dark purple; edible, with white pulp containing many small seeds; remains fleshy or dries and splits open; fruit ripens 2 months after flowering

short spines

russet flowers

taller, slim form

Habitat: desert scrub, desert grasslands, desert mountains, shortgrass prairies and oak woodlands between 2,300-8,900' (700-2,710 m); hills, flats, bajadas; volcanic rock, gravelly or silty soils

Range: far western and northwestern Texas, and isolated areas in the west central part of the state

**Green-flowered
Hedgehog**
rusty-spined form has
pale russet flowers
arising midstem

**Texas Rainbow
Hedgehog** (pg. 199)
resembles Green-flowered

**Texas Rainbow
Hedgehog** (pg. 199)
large flower just below the
stem tip

Compare: When not in flower, Texas Rainbow Hedgehog (pg. 199) is likely to be confused with Green-flowered Hedgehog. When blooming, Texas Rainbow blossoms are large and near the tip of the stem, while Green-flowered has small flowers that grow out from the stem, about midway up the sides.

Notes: Although always a small-sized hedgehog, Green-flowered is quite inconsistent in appearance across its range, occurring as a single stem or forming small clumps, and differing in the color and length of its spines as well as the color and fragrance of its flowers. There are eight distinctive forms in the state that hybridize freely where their ranges overlap. The variety for which the species is named occurs only in a small area of northwestern Texas and has lemon-scented, yellowish green flowers. This cold-hardy form is found as far north as Wyoming and South Dakota.

Three other varieties are more common and widespread in Texas. Common at middle elevations such as in the Davis Mountains, the taller, slim form has bands of short red and white spines and small, unscented, russet or yellow blooms that don't fully open. A longer-spined western form with yellowish brown flowers is easily seen in the Franklin Mountains near El Paso. The third variety, in Big Bend National Park, has pale russet flowers and rusty-tipped white spines.

spines

flower

fruit

ee page 354 for
larger map

Strawberry Hedgehog
Echinocereus stramineus

Size: H 4-12" (10-30 cm)

Shape: shaggy compact mounds, up to 3½' (1.1 m) wide, of 20-100 (can have up to 500) cylindrical stems; resembles a clump of straw

Stem: upright spiny stems; each stem, 2-4½" (5-11 cm) wide, has 10-16 (usually 12) somewhat wavy ribs with many long spines that mostly hide the green stem color, giving the plant a straggly appearance

Spines: straw-colored, tan or brown; ⅝-4" (1.5-10 cm) long; spines are somewhat translucent, turning white with age

Spine Clusters: overlapping, closely spaced spine clusters; each cluster has 2-4 straight central spines (lowest and longest projects straight outward) and 7-14 radial spines pointing in all directions

Flower: 1 to several funnel-shaped, magenta-to-red flowers on the sides of stems; each bloom, 4-5" (10-13 cm) wide, has layers of petals with darker bases around yellow and dark green flower parts

Blooming: late March-May; flowers partially close at night and reopen in the morning, lasting 1-4 days

Fruit: spiny round green pod, 2-2½" (5-6 cm) wide; when ripe turns strawberry red, spines are easy to brush off and has edible, sweet, pinkish white pulp that tastes like a strawberry; pulp contains many small black seeds

Habitat: desert mountains from 2,500-5,000' (760-1,525 m); hot sunny hillsides, limestone or volcanic bare rock outcrops, mesas, in canyons

Range: far western Texas

Strawberry Hedgehog
compact clumps
are shaggier

Pitaya (pg. 215)
dense mounds can look
like Strawberry Hedgehog

Pitaya (pg. 215)
stems have 6-9 ribs

Compare: Most closely resembles Pitaya (pg. 215), which can also form large mounds of stems, but Pitaya has smaller flowers. Strawberry Hedgehog appears even shaggier than Pitaya due to the close spacing of the many-spined circular areas (areoles), with the green color of the stems mostly obscured by the spines. Pitaya stems have 6-9 ribs, fewer than the usual dozen ribs of Strawberry.

Notes: A very spiny, shaggy hedgehog occurring only in the mountains of the Chihuahuan Desert region of far western Texas, southern New Mexico and northern Mexico. Forms large rounded mounds of stems that are the color of and look like stacks of straw from a distance. Also known as Strawpile or Straw-colored Hedgehog. Even the species name *stramineus* means "made of straw" in Latin.

Strawberry Hedgehog has large, showy flowers that are open all day, allowing bees to do most of the pollinating. The resulting fruit ripens a month later, the pods turn red and spines become easy to brush off. Abundant and harvested by American Indian tribes, the juicy fruit tastes like strawberry, for which this cactus is named. Produces the largest fruit of any hedgehog. The tiny seeds are rich in fat and provide nutrients to birds and rodents, which also eat the pulp.

spines

fruit

See page 354 for larger map

Scarlet Hedgehog
Echinocereus coccineus

Size: H 4-18" (10-45 cm)

Shape: loose cluster or dense mounds, up to 3' (.9 m) wide, of 20-100 (sometimes up to 500) cylindrical or round stems

Stem: multiple upright, light green stems, each 2-6" (5-15 cm) wide, with 5-14 vertical or wavy ribs with spines; ribs can sometimes have bumps (tubercles)

Spines: pale gray, yellow, red, brown or black, turning gray with age; ¹/₅-3¹/₄" (.5-8 cm) long

Spine Clusters: each cluster has up to 6 central spines (usually 1 outward-pointing and darker) and 1-18 radial spines pressed against the stem or pointing outward with the central spine; all spines are straight and look similar

Flower: 1 to several deep velvet red or red-orange flowers on the upper sides of stems; each goblet-shaped bloom, 1¹/₄-2³/₄" (3-7 cm) wide, has round-tipped petals with light bases around pinkish purple male flower parts (anthers)

Blooming: March-April, depending on elevation; blooms stay open 24 hours a day for over a week

Fruit: round, spiny, green or orangish red pod, ³/₄-1³/₈" (2-3.5 cm) long, has white pulp containing numerous small black seeds

Habitat: thorn scrub, grasslands and oak/juniper woodlands, and occasionally desert scrub, from 1,000-7,500' (305-2,285 m); open areas, among mesquite trees, rocky hilltops, mesas, canyons, slopes, cliffs, among boulders; volcanic or limestone soils

Range: far western and west central Texas

Scarlet Hedgehog
large mounds
resemble Pitaya

Pitaya *(pg. 215)*
slimmer, spinier stems

Pitaya *(pg. 215)*
pink, not red, flower

Compare: When not in bloom, large mounds of Pitaya (pg. 215) resemble those of Scarlet Hedgehog. Pitaya has more spines and slimmer stems than Scarlet. Scarlet Hedgehog is easy to identify when in bloom because no other Texas hedgehog has deep red or red-orange flowers.

Notes: Also known as Texas Claret-cup Hedgehog. Ranges from Arizona and New Mexico to Texas. One variety occurring only in Texas has fewer and shorter spines than does this species in other states. Hybridizes with Texas Rainbow Hedgehog (pg. 199) wherever their ranges overlap. Like other hedgehogs, Scarlet has very spiny fruit.

A large dense mound of Scarlet with the brilliant red flowers in full bloom is an amazing sight. Frequently cultivated due to its gorgeous blooms and its hardiness in different habitats. Unlike other hedgehogs, which are visited mainly by bees, this cactus is pollinated by hummingbirds. Attracted by flower color and copious nectar, a hummingbird fits its whole head into the flower, rather than just its bill. Most cacti produce flowers that have both male and female flower parts, but Scarlet Hedgehog plants have flowers with either male or female flower parts, not both.

spines

flower

fruit

ee page 354 for
larger map

CYLINDRICAL

Hedgehog

Pitaya

Echinocereus enneacanthus

Size: H 8-16" (20-40 cm)

Shape: loose or compact clumps, up to 3' (.9 m) wide, of 20-100 (can have up to 500) cylindrical stems

Stem: flabby, often sprawling, yellowish green stems; each stem, 1⅜-6" (3.5-15 cm) wide, has 6-9 ribs with short or long spines that do not obscure the stem

Spines: white, lavender gray or tan; ½-3½" (1-9 cm) long; sometimes tipped or banded with dark brown

Spine Clusters: widely spaced spine clusters; each cluster has 1-4 straight or curving stout central spines pointed outward and 5-10 (usually 9) radial spines pointing outward or downward

Flower: small cup-shaped magenta flowers on the sides of stems very near the tips; two forms, either 2" (5 cm) wide or 4" (10 cm) wide; both forms have 1 or more layers of petals with darker bases around yellow and green flower parts; flower buds are very spiny

Blooming: April-May; closing at night or when cloudy, blooms 2-4 days

Fruit: rounded, spiny, yellowish green pod, 1-1½" (2.5-4 cm) long, turns dull red or bronze when ripe; sweet, edible, pinkish white pulp smells and tastes like strawberry

short-spined form

spiny flower buds

Habitat: deserts, thorn scrub, plains, oak/juniper woodlands and desert mountains up to 5,100' (1,555 m); gravelly hillsides, bajadas, along rivers, under bushes; limestone or river-deposited soils

Range: far western, southern and south central Texas

Pitaya
spines are white, gray or tan and the green stems are visible

Strawberry Hedgehog
(pg. 207)
spines are straw-colored and cover the green stems

Strawberry Hedgehog
(pg. 207)
larger fruit

Compare: Pitaya and Strawberry Hedgehog (pg. 207) were once considered to be the same species. The long-spined form of Pitaya closely resembles Strawberry Hedgehog, which differs by having straw-colored spines that nearly totally obscure the green stems. The dull red or bronze fruit of Pitaya is smaller than the strawberry red fruit of Strawberry Hedgehog.

Notes: This sparsely spiny hedgehog has two forms—one is short-spined with thin stems and larger flowers, and is found mostly east of Big Bend; the other is long-spined with thick stems and smaller flowers, and ranges from Big Bend westward. The green color of the stems is partly to largely visible. Usually has nine radial spines, thus the species name *enneacanthus*, which is Greek for "nine thorns."

Tolerates a variety of habitats, occurring in the south central Texas plains or woodlands, far western deserts, among vegetation along the Rio Grande and in southern Texas thorn scrub. Sometimes referred to as Mexican Strawberry, this cactus has dull red or bronze fruit that tastes like strawberry, but is smaller than the fruit of the well-known Strawberry Hedgehog. Although the fruit is spiny, the spines are easily brushed off when ripe.

Can be cultivated, but needs well-drained soil and is sensitive to overwatering. Keep drier and cool in winter. Cold resistant, it can withstand freezing temperatures for short periods.

spines

immature fruit

Ladyfinger Hedgehog

Echinocereus pentalophus

e page 354 for
larger map

Size: H 4-24" (10-61 cm)

Shape: spreading clumps, up to 3' (.9 m) wide, of elongated, nearly square stems

Stem: freely branching, reclining long stems, each ½-2½" (1-6 cm) wide, green, red or purple with 4-5 ribs with sparse spines

Spines: tan, yellowish brown or ashy white to dark gray; also pale pink with dark tips; ¼-1⅜" (.6-3.5 cm) long

Spine Clusters: clusters of short straight rigid spines sparsely line each row; each cluster has 1 outward-pointing central spine (sometimes lacks a central spine) and 4-6 radial spines pressed against the stem

Flower: 1 to several funnel-shaped, dark pink blooms on the sides of stems near the tips; each large flower, 3-4" (7.5-10 cm) wide, has layers of petals with white or yellow bases and a center of pale yellow and green; buds are spiny

Blooming: March-April

Fruit: spiny oval green pod, ½-1" (1-2.5 cm) long, turns red and drops most of its spines when ripe and has white pulp containing many small seeds

Habitat: thorn scrub and pine/oak woodlands up to 500' (150 m); coastal plains

Range: southern Texas

Ladyfinger Hedgehog
nearly square stems with
4-5 crested ribs

Berlandier Hedgehog
(pg. 223)
cylindrical stems with 5-7
rows of tubercles

Berlandier Hedgehog
(pg. 223)
inner petals have red, not
white, bases

Compare: Often misidentified as the rare Berlandier Hedgehog (pg. 223), which has cylindrical stems with 5-7 rows of bumps (tubercles) rather than the 4-5 crested ribs of the nearly square Ladyfinger Hedgehog stems. Once classified as a variety of Berlandier, Ladyfinger also has shorter stems and forms smaller clumps. The white or yellow throats of its large pink flowers also distinguish this more common species from Berlandier, which has blossoms with dark pink throats.

Notes: A weak-stemmed hedgehog with elongated square stems lying partly on the ground with ends curving upright. The species name *pentalophus* comes from the Greek *penta* for "five" and *lophos* for "crest," referring to the ribs on the stems. In Texas, the name "Allicoche" is often used to refer to Ladyfinger and Berlandier Hedgehogs, as well as Allicoche Hedgehog (pg. 183).

Found only in Texas in the United States. Also native to eastern and northeastern Mexico, growing at low elevations in subtropical shrubby woodlands (thorn scrub) and in pine/oak woodlands at higher elevations.

Easily propagated by cutting a piece of stem during the summer, letting it dry for a couple of days and planting it in a pot. The stems branch readily, and soon you will have a mass of shoots. It blooms only for a week or two, but the large blossoms are a spectacular pink.

spines

Berlandier Hedgehog
Echinocereus berlandieri

ee page 354 for
larger map

Size: H 8-25" (20-64 cm)

Shape: spreading clumps, up to 10' (3 m) wide, of elongated cylindrical stems

Stem: freely branching, reclining long stems, each 1" (2.5 cm) wide, purple-tinged dark green with 5-7 rows of large bumps (tubercles) tipped with sparse spines

Spines: yellow-to-dark brown spines with brown tips; ½-2" (1-5 cm) long; aging to grayish white

Spine Clusters: clusters of straight rigid spines sparsely lined up in rows; each cluster has 1-3 outward-pointing central spines (longest central spine points downward) and 6-9 radial spines pressed against the stem

Flower: 1 to several funnel-shaped, dark pink blooms on the sides of stems near the tips; each large flower, 3-4" (7.5-10 cm) wide, has layers of pointed petals with darker pink bases and midstripes, and a center of pale yellow and green; buds are spiny

Blooming: May-June

Fruit: spiny, oval, olive green pod, ¾-1¼" (2-3 cm) long, turns red and drops most of its spines when ripe, white or clear pulp contains many small seeds

Habitat: mesquite thickets and grasslands up to 300' (90 m); coastal plains, shady thickets

Range: southern Texas near the Rio Grande, and an isolated area near the southeastern coast

Berlandier Hedgehog
pink flower has
dark throat

Ladyfinger Hedgehog
(pg. 219)
pink flower has
white throat

Ladyfinger Hedgehog
(pg. 219)
shorter, fewer spines

Compare: The flowers of Ladyfinger Hedgehog (pg. 219) look very much like Berlandier Hedgehog blossoms, but have dark pink instead of white throats. Ladyfinger stems are elongated like those of Berlandier, but Ladyfinger has fewer and shorter spines.

Notes: The elongated, branching stems of this clumping cactus are unlike the short stems of most hedgehogs. Discovered along the Nueces River in Texas in 1834. Named after French explorer Jean Louis Berlandier, who explored Mexico and settled in Texas in the mid-1800s. Rare in the wild, it is found mainly in the subtropical shrubby woodlands (thorn scrub) of southern Texas and northern Mexico.

Berlandier is often cultivated as an ornamental for its large, showy flowers, but only in very warm climates as it does not tolerate cold. This species does well with lots of rain. North of southern Texas and elsewhere in the United States, grow it in a pot in a greenhouse or as a houseplant. Indoors, it needs a location with short periods of direct sun and some indirect or filtered light. The stems elongate with age and when old enough, this cactus looks interesting in a hanging basket. Propagate from offshoots (called pups) of the cactus or from seed.

spines

flower

fruit

ee page 354 for larger map

CYLINDRICAL

Hedgehog

Dahlia Hedgehog
Echinocereus poselgeri

Size: H 12-24" (30-61 cm), sometimes up to 4' (1.2 m)

Shape: upright or climbing (can be sprawling), sparingly branching, very thin cylindrical stems

Stem: woody-looking stems, each ¼-½" (.6-1 cm) wide, with 8-10 shallow ribs covered with an interlacing network of spines

Spines: tan, brown or black; sometimes yellow, pink, white or gray; tiny spines, less than ½" (1 cm) long

Spine Clusters: clusters of many short slender spines densely line each row and interlace with spines from next cluster; each cluster has 1 (sometimes up to 3) dark central spine and 8-16 dark-tipped pale radial spines; all pressed closely against the stem

Flower: 1 to several funnel-shaped, dark rose pink blooms on stem tips; each flower, 1⅜-3" (3.5-7.5 cm) wide, has layers of petals with deep magenta mid-stripes around a center of dull yellow and green; buds are spiny

Blooming: March-April

Fruit: spiny, oval, dark green pod, 1" (2.5 cm) long, fleshy, drying to reddish brown and keeping its spines and wool when ripe; contains white pulp

Habitat: thorn scrub up to 650' (200 m); soils deposited by rivers
Range: southern Texas

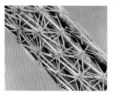

Dahlia Hedgehog
cylindrical stem with
shallow ribs and densely
interwoven spines

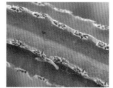

**Desert Night-blooming
Cereus** *(pg. 335)*
angular stem with
prominent ribs and widely
spaced, tiny spine clusters

Lace Hedgehog *(pg. 179)*
flower looks similar
to Dahlia Hedgehog

Compare: Dahlia Hedgehog stems look much like those of Desert Night-blooming Cereus (pg. 335) from a distance. The stems of both are very long and slender, and they are often seen leaning on branches in a shrub. However, Dahlia stems are cylindrical with shallow ribs covered with spines woven together in basket-like fashion, while Cereus stems have prominent ribs and sparse spine clusters. Dahlia flowers and fruit look a lot like those of Lace Hedgehog (pg. 179).

Notes: Looking little like a typical hedgehog, this elongated cactus with very slim stems grows upright, sprawls or intertwines with branches of a bush. Botanists classify plants by their flowers, fruit and seeds–not by the form of their leaves or stems, which can vary depending on the climate or habitat. Dahlia has been proven to belong to the hedgehog genus by its flowers and fruit, closely resembling those of Lace Hedgehog.

Uniquely among hedgehogs in the United States, the stems have a woody core that provides support. Slim stems seem to be a common characteristic of hedgehogs growing in thorn scrub, such as seen in Ladyfinger and Berlandier Hedgehogs (pp. 219 and 223, respectively). The long stems may be an adaptation enabling cacti to reach sunlight filtering through the canopy of leaves in subtropical woodlands.

Species name is for German cactus collector H. Poselger, who visited the Southwest and Mexico in the mid-1800s. Cactus cultivation is a popular hobby in Germany, which has no native cacti.

spines

fruit

Turk's Head Barrel
Ferocactus hamatacanthus

e page 355 for larger map

Size: H 4-24" (10-61 cm); W 3-12" (7.5-30 cm)

Shape: stout round or short cylindrical cactus; often grows in clumps

Stem: unbranched stem with 10-17 poorly defined rows of bumps (tubercles) or 13 prominent vertical ribs; lined with spines that mostly hide the green skin; deeply notched above each spine cluster

Spines: reddish brown or straw-colored spines, 1½-5" (4-13 cm) long

Spine Clusters: 12-16 spines per cluster; each cluster has 4-8 flexible smooth central spines, hooked or curved downward, sometimes flattened and papery; smaller slimmer spines are bristle-like

Flower: golden yellow flowers in a clump atop stem; each fragrant cup-shaped blossom, 2½-4" (6-10 cm) wide, has layers of pointed petals (outer petals have wide red midstripes) around a center of all-yellow flower parts

Blooming: June-August

Fruit: fleshy oblong green pod, ¾-2" (2-5 cm) long, spineless with scales on the skin and a tuft of leftover dry flower parts on top; turns deep red to reddish brown when ripe; contains very juicy, sweet white pulp with small seeds

immature plant

Habitat: desert scrub, thorn scrub and woodlands up to 7,500' (2,285 m); mesas, mountains, bajadas, valleys, under bushes, cracks in rocks; limestone or volcanic soils

Range: southern and far western Texas, as well as the southwestern border country between these two main areas

Turk's Head Barrel
red fruit is very juicy

Fishhook Barrel (pg. 235)
thick-walled yellow fruit
has dry interior

Fishhook Barrel (pg. 235)
orange-to-red flowers

Compare: The related Fishhook Barrel (pg. 235) has shorter spines and thick-walled yellow fruit that is dry inside, unlike the red fruit of Turk's Head, which is pulpy and juicy. Fishhook also has a ring of flowers that are more often orange or red, but can be yellow like Turk's Head blossoms.

Notes: A very spiny, stout barrel cactus with hooked or curved central spines that can be stout or papery, rounded or flattened. An immature plant covered with its protective, long, straw-colored spines looks more like a clump of dry grass than a cactus. *Hamatacanthus* means "hooked thorn" in Latin and refers to the largest central spine that is hooked or curved. The stem is topped with golden yellow flowers that can open anytime in the summer months. The flowers bloom for several days, opening about noon, partially closing at night and opening again the next day.

There are two varieties of Turk's Head. One is taller with large tubercles in poorly delineated rows and occurs in the Chihuahuan Desert and mountains of far western Texas. The other is smaller, has prominent, well-defined narrow ribs that are curved and is found in the subtropical shrubby woodlands (thorn scrub) of southern Texas. This variety is becoming rare as thorn scrub disappears due to agriculture. Although fairly widespread in western and southern Texas but not abundant, Turk's Head is found elsewhere in northern Mexico and in a tiny portion of southern New Mexico.

spines

flower

fruit

Fishhook Barrel
Ferocactus wislizeni

ee page 355 for larger map

Size: H 8-48" (20-122 cm), some are 8-10' (2.4-3 m); W 14-25" (36-64 cm)

Shape: stout round or cylindrical cactus with a flat top; taller plants lean southwest

Stem: single stem with 20-30 wide vertical ribs lined with spines that do not hide the green stem; ribs have a shallow notch above each spine cluster

Spines: dull red, gray, tan or white; 1½-5" (4-13 cm) long, some with dark tips

Spine Clusters: each cluster has 2-4 stout central spines (1 is hooked) with horizontal ridges and 6-16 flexible, bristle-like radial spines

Flower: orange, red or yellow flowers forming a wreath atop the stem; each cup-shaped blossom, 1½-3½" (4-9 cm) wide, has layers of petals with darker midstripes and a center of yellow and orange flower parts

Blooming: June-August, after summer rains begin; flowering occurs later than most other cacti

Fruit: fleshy oval green pod, 1⅜-2½" (3.5-6 cm) long, spineless with scales on the skin and a brown tuft of leftover dry flower parts on top, turns bright yellow when ripe and releases small black seeds through a pore in the base

Habitat: desert scrub, grasslands and lower elevation oak woodlands between 3,500-5,300' (1,065-1,615 m); bajadas, rocky hillsides, canyons; gravelly soils

Range: restricted to the Franklin Mountains in far western Texas and near a few historic settlements in Big Bend National Park

Fishhook Barrel
immature Fishhooks
have fewer ribs than
mature plants

Turk's Head Barrel
(pg. 231)
longer, messier spines

Eagle's Claw Cactus
(pg. 167)
only 8 ribs and bluish
green stems

Compare: Young Fishhook Barrels have fewer ribs than when mature and can resemble Turk's Head Barrel (pg. 231) or Eagle's Claw Cactus (pg. 167). Turk's Head has much longer, messier spines than Fishhook. Eagle's Claw has eight ribs and a bluish green stem; an immature Fishhook has more than eight ribs and a yellowish green stem.

Notes: Barrel cacti are named for their shape and possibly for the mistaken belief that they are hollow and contain water. In the rainy season, the vertical ribs widen and become shallower, allowing the cactus to expand as the plant absorbs water. Storing water enables it to survive many months without rain. If a desperately thirsty desert hiker manages the difficult task of cutting one open, the thick liquid pulp can be consumed, but it has a foul taste and may cause vomiting.

The largest barrel cactus in the U.S., Fishhook is a stout green cactus with reddish gray spines that glow bright red when they get wet. Named for the large, hooked central spine once used to catch fish. The leathery fruit doesn't contain pulp and is usually not eaten by people. Fruit stays on the plant until the next year.

Although limited in Texas to the far west, this cactus is abundant in Arizona, New Mexico and northern Mexico. Young Fishhooks, which have stouter spines than mature plants, start out round and do not lengthen until they attain a width of 12 inches (30 cm). Sometimes older plants over 8 feet (2.4 m) tall tilt southwest so much that the whole cactus uproots and falls over.

spines

fruit

Cockspur Prickly Pear
Opuntia pusilla

Prickly Pear

ee page 355 for larger map

Size: H 1-4" (2.5-10 cm)

Shape: low-growing, trailing cactus forming loose clumps of thick or flattened, oval or elongated, segmented stems

Stem: multiple green stem segments (pads); each pad, 1-2" (2.5-5 cm) long, ½-1" (1-2.5 cm) wide and often nearly as thick as wide; pads are knobby, easily detached and turn reddish green with stress

Spines: reddish brown spines, aging to gray; up to 1¼" (3 cm) long

Spine Clusters: rows of 2-5 circular areas (areoles) across each pad; each areole with tan-to-gray wool and 1-2 stout straight barbed spines per cluster; crescents of short, hair-like, yellow-to-brown spines (glochids) above each cluster

Flower: all-yellow flowers upright on pads; each blossom, 2-2½" (5-6 cm) wide, has a single, widely spreading layer of broad petals around a center of white and yellow flower parts

Blooming: April-May, sporadically from August-October

Fruit: spineless barrel-shaped pod, 1-1½" (2.5-4 cm) long, is fleshy, turning glossy and bright red when ripe; contains sweet red pulp with tan seeds

Habitat: coastal sand dunes and pinewoods up to 50' (15 m); barren sandy areas, rocky outcrops

Range: limited to along the coast in southeastern Texas

Cockspur Prickly Pear
sprawling or creeping
plant with small,
thick pads

Brittle Prickly Pear
(pg. 243)
plant looks similar
to Cockspur

Brittle Prickly Pear
(pg. 243)
red and yellow
flower parts

Compare: Brittle Prickly Pear (pg. 243) has thick pads shaped like those of Cockspur Prickly Pear and unlike most other prickly pears in Texas. Brittle is limited to northwestern Texas and does not overlap in range with Cockspur. Brittle flowers have red and yellow flower parts and a double layer of petals, while Cockspur blooms are white and yellow in the center and have a single layer of widely spreading petals.

Notes: A low-growing, spiny prickly pear found only along the Gulf coast from southeastern Texas to the northern half of Florida, inland through Florida to the Atlantic, and north along the coast to North Carolina. Common on the barrier islands off the coast of the Carolinas. Also called Dune Prickly Pear, this small cactus grows only on sand dunes or in pine scrub.

The small, thick oval pads grow temporary leaves that are conical and tinged red. As the pads elongate with age, the tiny leaves fall off and are replaced by needle-like spines that are long and stout with tiny hooked barbs. The pads readily break off the plant if the spines become embedded in shoes or flesh. These barbed spines are painfully difficult to remove from skin.

Thought to be closely related to Eastern Prickly Pear (pg. 259), which is much less spiny and has flatter, thinner pads. Cockspur plants are surprisingly cold hardy.

spines

flower

immature fruit

ee page 355 for
larger map

Brittle Prickly Pear
Opuntia fragilis

Size: H 1-4" (2.5-10 cm)

Shape: low-growing dense mats, 12-20" (30-50 cm) wide, of globe-shaped, cylindrical or flat segmented stems

Stem: up to hundreds of stem segments (pads); each pad, $\frac{1}{2}$-$2\frac{1}{4}$" (1-5.5 cm) long, $\frac{1}{2}$-1" (1-2.5 cm) wide and often nearly as thick as wide; pads are knobby and easily detached

Spines: yellow, brown or gray with brown tips; $\frac{1}{3}$-$\frac{9}{10}$" (.8-2.4 cm) long

Spine Clusters: diagonal rows of 3-5 clusters across the pad; 3-8 barbed spines per cluster with 1-3 downward-curving spines and inconspicuous crescents of short hair-like brown spines (glochids); clusters are surrounded by woolly white circles

Flower: 1-2 pale greenish yellow flowers atop the upper edges of pads; each bloom, 1-2" (2.5-5 cm) wide, has overlapping, spoon-shaped petals around pale yellow and red flower parts

Blooming: April-June, over a period of several weeks, but blooms only rarely

Fruit: somewhat spiny, fleshy, reddish green pod, drying to tan when ripe, $\frac{1}{2}$-$\frac{3}{4}$" (1-2 cm) long, containing tan seeds

woolly white circles

Habitat: grasslands up to 4,700' (1,435 m); among sagebrush, barren sandy areas

Range: limited to northwestern Texas (north of Amarillo), especially along the Canadian River

Brittle Prickly Pear
potato-shaped or thick
pads, not flat like other
prickly pear pads

Potts Prickly Pear (pg. 251)
some young prickly pears
look like Brittle

Common Dog Cholla
(pg. 307)
thick stem segments
resemble Brittle pads

Compare: Brittle Prickly Pear has thick pads, unlike most other prickly pears in Texas, but can superficially resemble other species of young prickly pears such as Potts Prickly Pear (pg. 251). Brittle pads look most like the thick, segmented stems of the low-growing dog chollas, just not as spiny.

Notes: A low-growing prickly pear that blooms infrequently. Flowers are found on it most often when it grows in association with lichens. A lichen cover keeps moisture in the soil, helping flowers to bloom. To propagate, it relies more on the growth of fallen pads rather than its blossoms.

Sometimes called Potato Cactus for the potato-like shape of the segmented stems. *Fragilis* refers to the pads, which detach easily. These spiny pieces cling to the fur of passing animals and root wherever they drop to the ground, forming new plants. When bison ranged over much of North America, they probably spread this cactus by carrying the pads or fruit on their woolly coats.

Found in the western half of this country in more than 20 states. Ranges farther north than any other cactus species, extending into Canada as far as northern Alberta and British Columbia, where winter temperatures dip to -50°F (-46°C). The low mats and thick pads allow this unusual cactus to survive in extreme cold. The mats are quickly covered and insulated by snow, while the thick pads reduce the ratio of surface area to volume, thus reducing heat loss.

spines

fruit

ee page 355 for
larger map

Plains Prickly Pear
Opuntia polyacantha

Size: H 4-10" (10-25 cm)

Shape: low-growing spreading mats, 12-36'" (30-91 cm) wide, of broadly paddle-shaped, flat segmented stems

Stem: multiple yellowish green stem segments (pads); each densely spiny pad, 2¾-5" (7-13 cm) long and 2¼-4½" (5.5-11 cm) wide, is firmly attached

Spines: white to gray to reddish brown, ½-2¾" (1-7 cm) long

Spine Clusters: diagonal rows of 6-11 closely spaced clusters across nearly the entire pad; 6-17 slender spines per cluster with 1-3 longer spines pointing out and down; spines sometimes long, curling and thread-like near bases of older pads; inconspicuous crescent of hair-like yellow spines (glochids) above each cluster

Flower: 1 to several all-yellow blossoms atop upper edges of pads; each cup-shaped flower, 1½-2" (4-5 cm) wide, with spoon-shaped petals around a center of yellow and green flower parts

Blooming: early May-June

Fruit: egg-shaped spiny pod, drying to tan when ripe, ¾-1½" (2-4 cm) long, containing pale tan or white seeds

Habitat: deserts, grasslands and mountain oak/juniper woodlands between 3,600-8,300' (1,100-2,530 m); among grasses or low trees, on flats and slopes; clay, sandy or gravelly soils

Range: west of the Pecos River in far western Texas and in a few counties in northwestern Texas

Plains Prickly Pear
one variety looks more like
a dog cholla

Plains Prickly Pear
spinier, smaller pads

**Brown-spine Prickly
Pear** *(pg. 263)*
longer, wider pads and
fewer spines

Compare: An unusual variety of Plains Prickly Pear that occurs in the Rio Grande Valley near El Paso looks like a dog cholla more than it resembles other prickly pears. Brown-spine Prickly Pear (pg. 263) overlaps in range, but has fewer spines and larger pads than Plains.

Notes: Cold tolerant, the hardy Plains Prickly Pear grows throughout western North America from British Columbia and Saskatchewan in Canada, south to Texas and Arizona. In winter, the pads become very wrinkled as cells in the skin lose water, concentrating the salts and other chemicals that are in the sap. This concentrated sap acts like antifreeze in a vehicle radiator, lowering the temperature at which the cells would freeze and suffer damage.

The species name *polyacantha* means "many thorns" in Latin. During drought when grass availability is limited, ranchers will sometimes burn off the cactus spines so their livestock can feed on the pads. Pads sprout roots on the lower edges wherever they touch the ground, giving this spreading cactus its ability to propagate in low dense mats of vegetation that cover large areas.

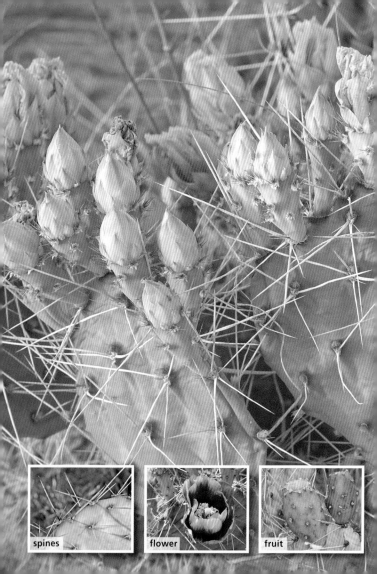

spines

flower

fruit

e page 355 for
larger map

SEGMENTED

Prickly Pear

Potts Prickly Pear
Opuntia pottsii

Size: H 8-12" (20-30 cm)

Shape: small shrub, less than 24" (61 cm) wide, of upright flat segmented stems

Stem: 6-10 heart- to diamond-shaped stem segments (pads); each dull green or bluish green pad, 2" (5 cm) long and 1½-3" (4-7.5 cm) wide, with spines only on the upper half of pad; some pads can be up to 5" (13 cm) long

Spines: grayish white, sometimes reddish brown; 1½-2½" (4-6 cm) long; sometimes spineless

Spine Clusters: diagonal rows of 4-6 clusters only on the upper third of pads; 1-4 slender spines per cluster with hair-like, yellow-to-brownish red spines (glochids) in sparse or dense short tufts

Flower: 8-11 all-red or reddish yellow flowers atop the upper edges of pads; each cup-shaped blossom, 2½" (6 cm) wide, has all-red petals or inner yellow petals tinged with red, around yellow flower parts; flower buds are peach-colored

Blooming: April-June, but mostly mid-May, over a period of 1 week

Fruit: oval fleshy pod, green to yellow to dull red, 1-1½" (2.5-4 cm) long, with few spines or spineless; containing juicy, pale green pulp with tan seeds

Habitat: grasslands in river bottomlands between 2,800-5,500' (855-1,675 m); flats, hills; sandy to loamy soils

Range: western Texas mostly west of the Pecos River, but also in a few counties just northeast of the Pecos River

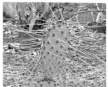

Potts Prickly Pear
white spines only on
upper half of smaller pads

Brown-spine Prickly Pear *(pg. 263)*
larger plant and
larger pads

Black-spine Prickly Pear *(pg. 267)*
much longer spines

Compare: Resembles Brown-spine Prickly Pear (pg. 263), but Potts is smaller overall and has lots of grayish white spines on its smaller pads. Also similar to Black-spine Prickly Pear (pg. 267), but Black-spine is somewhat larger and has much longer spines.

Notes: Stems of all prickly pears grow in jointed segments (pads) and have spine clusters with many minute barbed bristles (glochids) as well as spines. Glochids are present only on prickly pear, dog cholla and cholla cacti. Each new pad grows from a spine cluster on an old pad, starting as a bud displaying tiny ephemeral leaves. Prickly pear cacti are sometimes called flat-stemmed opuntias. This distinguishes them from the chollas, which are known as round-stemmed opuntias.

Potts is one of the smallest prickly pears, with upright pads growing from a single vertical stem, tuberous roots containing milky white juice and spines that often twist spirally. Once thought to be a variety of Western Prickly Pear (pg. 255), which is widespread in Texas east of the Pecos River. Potts is one of two prickly pears in Texas that can have all-red or yellow flowers, but plants with magenta, pink and orange flowers have also been seen.

Potts is common in far western Texas, southeastern Arizona, southern New Mexico and Chihuahua, Mexico. Isolated plants have been found as far northeast as Missouri.

spines

flower

immature fruit

Prickly Pear

Western Prickly Pear
Opuntia macrorhiza

e page 356 for
larger map

Size: H 6-14" (10-36 cm)

Shape: low-growing, spreading clumps, 3-5' (.9-1.5 m) wide, of round or egg-shaped flat segmented stems that are firmly attached; pads become flabby and wrinkled during drought or cold

Stem: multiple bluish or grayish green stem segments (pads); each thick pad, 2-4½" (5-11 cm) long and 1⅜-3" (3.5-7.5 cm) wide, can have 1-4 spines on the outer portions of pads or can be spineless; pads turn purplish green in winter

Spines: white or yellow, 1-2½" (2.5-6 cm) long, with reddish brown bases

Spine Clusters: diagonal rows of 5-6 circular areas (areoles) across pads; spineless or with clusters of 1-4 upright, spreading or downward-pointing spines on outer portion of each pad; each cluster has tan wool and pale yellow, tan or reddish brown hair-like spines (glochids) in dense tufts and crescents

Flower: apricot-to-yellow and red blossoms on upper edges of pads; each cup-shaped flower, 2-3" (5-7.5 cm) wide, has broad petals with obvious red bases around a wide center of yellow and white or pale green flower parts

Blooming: April-June

Fruit: fleshy slim egg-shaped pod, 1-1½" (2.5-4 cm) long, with few glochids; turns yellowish green to purplish red when ripe, contains tan seeds and has clear juice that tastes like sour apple; ripens 2-3 months after blooming

Habitat: chaparral, prairies and grassy pine woodlands up to 3,000' (915 m); usually in grassy areas; dry, limestone and sandy soils

Range: broad band from northwestern to southeastern Texas and extending into southern Texas along the coast; ranges over about two-thirds of the state

Western Prickly Pear
yellow flowers with
red bases

Potts Prickly Pear (pg. 251)
can have all-red flowers

Potts Prickly Pear (pg. 251)
smaller pads, forms
smaller clumps

Compare: Potts Prickly Pear (pg. 251) was once thought to be a variety of Western Prickly Pear. In Texas, Potts can have all-red flowers as well as yellow flowers with red bases like Western. Potts has smaller pads and forms smaller clumps than Western.

Notes: Closely related to Eastern Prickly Pear (pg. 259), Western Prickly Pear is a low, clump-forming small cactus with flattened pads that are bluish green. Grows mainly in the grasslands of the Great Plains of North America. Also called Plains Prickly Pear, but is not the Plains Prickly Pear on pg. 247. Ranges from Colorado and Kansas to Missouri, south through Texas and into New Mexico.

Sometimes called Tuberous-rooted Prickly Pear for its thick roots, which are also referred to by the species name *macrorhiza*, meaning "large root" in Greek. Tolerant of drought due to its succulent, water-storing pads and tuberous roots. Western Prickly Pear populations increase in number during dry spells and decrease when wet conditions favor the growth of grasses.

Pronghorn, deer, jackrabbits and turtles eat the fleshy fruit and help distribute the seeds. During periods of drought, ranchers have singed off the spines and fed the pads to their cattle.

spines

immature fruit

Eastern Prickly Pear
Opuntia humifusa

ee page 356 for
larger map

Size: H 6-20" (15-50 cm)

Shape: low-growing or upright spreading clumps, 12-18" (30-45 cm) wide, of segmented flat stems that are round, egg-shaped or oblong

Stem: multiple bright green stem segments (pads); each thick pad, 2-7" (5-18 cm) long and 1½-5" (4-13 cm) wide; pads turn purplish green in winter

Spines: often spineless or when present, white to brown; 1-2½" (2.5-6 cm) long

Spine Clusters: diagonal rows of 4-6 round areas (areoles) are spineless or with 1-2 stout spreading spines per cluster; each cluster has tan or brown wool, and dense tufts and crescents of hair-like, dark yellow-to-reddish brown spines (glochids)

Flower: bright all-yellow blossoms on upper edges of pads; each widely cup-shaped flower, 3-4" (7.5-10 cm) wide, has broad petals around a wide center of yellow and white flower parts

Blooming: April-June

Fruit: fleshy club-shaped pod, 1-2" (2.5-5 cm) long, has few glochids; turns brownish red when ripe; sour green pulp or sweet red pulp contains tan seeds; fruit tastes like watermelon

Habitat: open pine woodlands, prairies and savannahs up to 500' (150 m); dunes, open grassy areas, rock outcrops, along streams; among oak and juniper trees; dry sandy soils

Range: eastern Texas

Eastern Prickly Pear
flower with some red at
petal bases, but usually
all yellow

Western Prickly Pear
(pg. 255)
more red at bases and up
the midveins of petals

Western Prickly Pear
(pg. 255)
can have more spines

Compare: Western Prickly Pear (pg. 255), which overlaps in a small portion of its range with Eastern Prickly Pear, is easily confused with and was once thought to be a variety of Eastern. Western flowers have red bases, but Eastern blooms are usually all yellow. Western has 1-4 spines in each cluster on the outer parts of the pads, whereas Eastern is more often spineless or has 1-2 spines per cluster.

Notes: Eastern Prickly Pear is one of the most widespread of prickly pear cacti, covering most of the United States east of the Rocky Mountains and ranging into Ontario, Canada. This is the only native cactus found in some eastern states. Oddly, the pads mostly face east. Often called Hardy Prickly Pear due to its tolerance for a wide range of climates and habitats.

Species name *humifusa,* derived from Latin words meaning "earth" and "spread," refers to its sprawling growth form. The pads dry out and shrivel during fall in preparation for winter–retreating even closer to ground level. In Florida, however, this cactus forms upright small trees or shrubs as tall as 6¹/₂ feet (2 m).

Prickly Pear cactus fruit (called *las tunas* in Spanish) are very popular worldwide. Used to make candy and jams, the yearly commercial production of prickly pear fruit is twice that of strawberries. American Indians ate the fruit fresh, stewed or dried. The juice was used to treat warts, and cut stems were used for treatment of rattlesnake bites or bound onto wounds.

spines

flower

fruit

e page 356 for
larger map

SEGMENTED

Prickly Pear

Brown-spine Prickly Pear

Opuntia phaeacantha

Size: H 12-27½" (30-70 cm)

Shape: low-growing, sprawling or prostrate clumps, 3-8' (.9-2.4 m) wide, of paddle-shaped, broadly egg-shaped or circular segmented stems; stems can be wrinkled

Stem: multiple light green-to-bluish green stem segments (pads); each pad, 2½-10" (6-25 cm) long and 3-8" (7.5-20 cm) wide, is flat and weakly attached; sometimes purple on pad edges and around spine clusters, especially in winter

Spines: reddish brown, brown and white, or white to gray; 1-3" (2.5-7.5 cm) long; some with brown tips and bases

Spine Clusters: diagonal rows of 5-9 clusters across pad; each cluster with 1-10 straight, curved or twisted spines (longer and denser on upper half to two-thirds of pad, no spines or a few shorter ones lower on pad); dense, hair-like, yellow or brown spines (glochids) in tufts at top of each cluster and on pad edges

Flower: 1 to several yellow blooms (sometimes pink or salmon), turning orange, atop upper edges of pads; each tulip-shaped bloom, 2-2½" (5-6 cm) wide, has petals with red bases and wavy edges around pale yellow, reddish yellow and white flower parts

Blooming: April-June, over a period of several weeks

Fruit: barrel-shaped, red-to-purple pod, 1-2" (2.5-5 cm) long, few spines or spineless, with reddish brown glochids at the base of pod; bright red, pink or pale green pulp is edible, containing large tan seeds

SEGMENTED STEMS, **Prickly Pear 263**

trailing pads

cochineal insect webs

Habitat: grasslands, mountain basins and oak/juniper woodlands between 800-7,500' (245-2,285 m), more rarely in deserts below 4,000' (1,220 m); open areas, plains, rocky hillsides, rock crevices, along washes, valleys, in canyons among grasses or creosote bushes; volcanic or limestone, sandy to gravelly well-drained soils

Range: central, northwestern and far western Texas

Brown-spine Prickly Pear
shorter spines on upper part of pad only

Brown-spine Prickly Pear
can have many more glochids

Black-spine Prickly Pear
(pg. 267)
longer spines, fewer glochids

Compare: Brown-spine Prickly Pear has shorter spines and more numerous hair-like spines (glochids) than the similar Black-spine Prickly Pear (pg. 267).

Notes: Sometimes considered several separate species, this is a very widespread, common cactus across the West from California to Kansas and Oklahoma, and into Mexico. In Texas, these plants can have more white spines than are found on this species in other states. The tulip shape of the flower gives this cactus another name, Tulip Prickly Pear. Also called Sprawling Prickly Pear for its habit of trailing along the ground, with pads rooting wherever they touch the soil, forming chains of plants. Newly sprouted during the summer monsoons, the pads are first red, turning green with age.

Prickly pear fruit and pads are high in pectin, which may lower cholesterol in humans, and are also high in slowly absorbed soluble fibers that help keep blood sugar in diabetics stable. A parasitic cochineal insect can infest prickly pears, covering the pads with cottony white webs. Carminic acid, extracted from the insects to make a bright red dye (carmine), is used to color food, drugs and cosmetics.

spines

flower

fruit

e page 356 for
larger map

Black-spine Prickly Pear
Opuntia macrocentra

Size: H 12-36" (30-91 cm)

Shape: low-growing shrub, 2-4' (61-122 cm) wide, of upright or reclining, broad paddle-shaped or circular segmented stems

Stem: multiple bluish green stem segments (pads) with a tinge of purple on edges and around spine clusters; each flattened pad, 3-8" (7.5-20 cm) long and 2½-7" (6-18 cm) wide; entire pad turns nearly red during cold or drought

Spines: spineless or 2-5" (5-13 cm) long, reddish brown to black (sometimes yellow) with white tips; long spines turning chalky white to gray with age

Spine Clusters: diagonal rows of 6-8 clusters across upper quarter to half of each pad, or only on the upper edges; up to 3 thin flexible spines per cluster, with longest spine pointed conspicuously upward; some clusters have reddish brown or yellow, hair-like spines (glochids) in short crescent-shaped pointed tufts

Flower: yellow and red flowers atop the upper edges of pads; each cup-shaped bloom, 2-3" (5-7.5 cm) wide, with lower inner half of petals tinged dark red around pale yellow and green flower parts

Blooming: April-May, over a period of several weeks

Fruit: barrel-shaped, red or purple pod, 1-1½" (2.5-4 cm) long, smooth, spineless and fleshy, with pale purple-to-clear pulp containing tan seeds

Habitat: deserts and grasslands from 3,000-5,000' (915-1,525 m); flats, hills, valleys; sandy to rocky soils

Range: far western Texas, from the Mexico and New Mexico borders east to the Pecos River

Black-spine Prickly Pear
longer, darker spines on
upper pad

**Brown-spine Prickly
Pear** (pg. 263)
shorter, lighter spines

Big Bend Prickly Pear
(pg. 271)
can have even
longer spines

Compare: Resembles Brown-spine Prickly Pear (pg. 263), but Black-spine Prickly Pear has longer, darker spines. Also resembles Big Bend Prickly Pear (pg. 271), but that cactus can have even longer spines.

Notes: A short shrub with thin flexible spines and deep yellow and red flowers that do not open as widely as the blossoms of other prickly pears. Often called Long-spine Prickly Pear for the length of its spines–among the longest of any cactus species in Texas. The species name *macrocentra* refers to the longest central spine in the uppermost spine clusters. Interestingly, there is a Black-spine variety that lacks spines.

The pads are bluish green with tinges of purple on the edges during monsoon rains, but when stressed by cold or drought, the entire pad will turn nearly red. The yellow and red flowers or red fruit against the purple and green or red pads, combined with the compact growth of this small cactus, make it an attractive choice for cultivation to desert landscapers.

Although Black-spine Prickly Pear extends into Mexico, in the United States it is found only in Texas, southeastern Arizona and southern New Mexico.

spines

flower

immature fruit

ee page 356 for
larger map

Big Bend Prickly Pear
Opuntia azurea

Size: H 12-40" (30-102 cm)

Shape: low-growing, open or compact, sprawling or upright shrub, 2-4' (61-122 cm) wide, branching from the base or with a short trunk, with broad circular or egg-shaped segmented stems

Stem: multiple reddish purple or yellowish green stem segments (pads); each pad, 3-8" (7.5-20 cm) long and 3-8" (7.5-20 cm) wide, is flattened; purple color increases in drought or cold

Spines: all black, reddish brown, or black (sometimes yellow or light brown) with outer half white or white tips; 2-6¾" (5-17 cm) long; turning white to gray with age; sometimes spineless

Spine Clusters: diagonal rows of 3-5 circular areas (areoles) across each pad; 1-12 dark spines in clusters on the upper quarter to half of each pad or only on the upper edges; spines are very long, thin and flexible; clusters lack hair-like spines (glochids)

Flower: yellow-and-red flowers atop the upper edges of pads; each bloom, 2-3" (5-7.5 cm) wide, is cup-shaped with lower half of petals tinged dark red; pale yellow and green flower parts; turning pink to apricot with age

Blooming: March-June, over a period of several weeks

Fruit: oval or cylindrical green pod, 1-1½" (2.5-4 cm) long, ripens to red or purple, is smooth, spineless and fleshy; pale green-to-clear pulp is sweet and contains tan seeds

Habitat: desert to mountain grasslands between 1,600-5,500' (490-1,675 m); flats, hills, valleys; sandy to rocky soils

Range: Big Bend region of far western Texas

Big Bend Prickly Pear
longer spines

Black-spine Prickly Pear
(pg. 267)
spines not quite as long

Black-spine Prickly Pear
(pg. 267)
usually more areoles

Compare: Black-spine Prickly Pear (pg. 267) very closely resembles Big Bend Prickly Pear. However, Black-spine longest spines are not as long as those of Big Bend, and Black-spine has 6-8 circular areas (areoles) in each diagonal row across the pads, whereas Big Bend usually has 3-5 areoles per row.

Notes: Big Bend Prickly Pear is a variable species. Its stem color depends upon its habitat and the season. It can be reddish purple or lavender, turning more purple during drought or winter. While the stem is not always purple, this cactus is also known as Purple Prickly Pear. The stem can also be bluish or dark green, or dull grayish green with purple rings around each areole or with purple pad edges. The species name *azurea* is Latin for "blue," referring to one of its many shades.

Prickly pear cacti are very important in Mexico as a source of cattle fodder, and the pads and fruit are also grown as food for humans. However, prickly pears imported into Australia and other parts of the world have become a major problem, turning weedy and taking over large areas. In Australia, Cactus Moths have been used successfully to control prickly pear populations. Unfortunately, these previously beneficial moths have attacked native prickly pear cacti in Florida and are posing a serious threat to cactus crops in Mexico and native prickly pears in Texas.

spines

flower

fruit

página 356 for
larger map

see page 356 for larger map

Marblefruit Prickly Pear
Opuntia strigil

Size: H 20-40" (50-102 cm)

Shape: upright, densely compact shrub, 2-6' (.6-1.8 m) wide, with spreading branches of many flat segmented stems

Stem: dark-spotted, dull greenish yellow stem segments (pads); each pad, 4-6¾" (10-17 cm) long and 3½-5¾" (9-14.5 cm) wide, is oval or circular with spines spread evenly across the firmly attached pad

Spines: dark reddish brown with pale yellow tips; ½-1½" (1-4 cm) long; spines turning black and white with age

Spine Clusters: diagonal rows of 7-10 clusters across the pad; 7-13 straight spines per cluster, varying greatly in size, with 1 longest, stoutest central spine; all spines point downward and sprout from the lower half of the cluster; each cluster has dark gray-black wool and hair-like yellow spines (glochids)

Flower: creamy yellow flowers on the upper edges of pads; each tulip-shaped bloom, 2-2½" (5-6 cm) wide, with petals tinged reddish yellow at their bases around pale yellow flower parts

Blooming: early April-June

Fruit: small rounded fleshy pod, ⅝-1" (1.5-2.8 cm) long; spineless, but with many glochids concentrated on upper rim; green, turning rose-colored when ripe with somewhat dry, pale green pulp containing tan seeds

Habitat: desert scrub from 2,400-4,600' (730-1,400 m); mesas, canyons, slopes, shallow soil in limestone rock crevices

Range: western Texas, bordering counties on both the west and east sides of the Pecos River

Marblefruit Prickly Pear
looks like Blind Prickly Pear
from a distance

Blind Prickly Pear (pg. 287)
resembles Marblefruit
from afar

Blind Prickly Pear (pg. 287)
spineless pads

Compare: The round greenish yellow pads and dark circular areas (areoles) of Marblefruit Prickly Pear could cause it to be easily mistaken from a distance for a small, squat version of Blind Prickly Pear (pg. 287). Upon closer inspection, however, the evenly spaced spines on Marblefruit pads distinguish it from the spineless pads of Blind.

Notes: A small, spreading prickly pear with densely packed, round pads that are evenly spiny. Has the smallest fruit of any prickly pear in Texas–about the size of a marble and nearly round. Even though attractive, the pinkish red fruit (ripening in July) is not juicy or sweet. The species name *strigil* is Latin for "skin brush," referring to the resemblance of the very spiny pads to instruments historically used by bathing Romans to scrape their skin. Also known as Bearded Prickly Pear because the spines sprouting from the edges of the greenish yellow pads cause them to appear to be encircled by a reddish brown ring.

Extremely limited in range in the United States. Found only in Texas and south into Coahuila, Mexico. Although not common, this spiny little cactus is seen most frequently in the Texas counties of Pecos and Terrell. Sometimes cultivated, usually grown from a cutting. Allow the cut end of a pad to dry and seal over before planting. The small size makes it appropriate for growing in pots on desert patios.

spines

flower

fruit

Border Prickly Pear
Opuntia atrispina

ee page 357 for
larger map

Size: H 20-40" (50-102 cm)

Shape: spreading sprawling shrub, 4-6' (1.2-1.8 m) wide, of circular or egg-shaped, segmented flat stems

Stem: multiple pale yellowish green stem segments (pads); each pad, 4-6" (10-15 cm) long and 3-5" (7.5-13 cm) wide, is densely dotted with dark brown ringed by reddish purple; spines on upper portion of pads

Spines: reddish brown to black with yellow tips; ¹/₂-1³/₈" (1-3.5 cm) long

Spine Clusters: diagonal rows of 5-7 clusters; 1-2 largest central spines per cluster are black to reddish brown with yellow on outer half and pointing upward; 1-3 much shorter gray spines pointing downward; each cluster has tan wool and dense tufts of hair-like, dark yellow-to-brown spines (glochids)

Flower: pale yellow blossoms on upper edges of pads, turning apricot or salmon-colored with age; each loosely cup-shaped flower, 1-3" (2.5-7.5 cm) wide, has broad outer petals with a pinkish brown midstripe and inner petals with green bases, around a pale cream-colored center

Blooming: April, perhaps May

Fruit: conical fleshy spineless pod, up to 1" (2.5 cm) long, green turning bright red to reddish yellow when ripe, few glochids, greenish yellow pulp inside contains tan or gray seeds

Habitat: grasslands from 1,000-2,100' (305-640 m); shrublands, mesas, canyons, hills; limestone, sandy or gravelly soils

Range: west central Texas along the border with Mexico

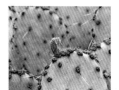

Border Prickly Pear
spines on upper part
of pad

Marblefruit Prickly Pear
(pg. 275)
spinier across entire pad

Marblefruit Prickly Pear
(pg. 275)
rounded fruit

Compare: Border Prickly Pear is similar to Marblefruit Prickly Pear (pg. 275) in spine color. Unlike Border, Marblefruit has spines distributed across the entire pad and has rounded fruit.

Notes: This sprawling prickly pear is recognizable mainly by its distinctly two-toned, reddish brown or black and yellow central spines. Also can be distinguished by its flowering habit, which is extremely early in the spring, as compared to other cacti. The blooms open early in April, covering the plant with yellow and salmon-colored flowers. Another common name for this cactus is Black-and-yellow-spine Prickly Pear. Looks similar to and may actually be a variety of the closely related Marblefruit Prickly Pear.

The range of this low-growing cactus is severely limited, although it can be common where it occurs. "Border" in the common name is for the proximity of its range to the Mexico border. Found only in a small area that stretches along a portion of U.S. Highway 90 from the Anacacho Mountains in Uvalde County, west through the mountains by the Devils and Pecos Rivers, to near Dryden, Texas. It occurs only in Texas in the United States, but is also found in Mexico.

glochids

flower

fruit

ee page 357 for
larger map

Chenille Prickly Pear
Opuntia aciculata

Size: H 2-4' (61-122 cm)

Shape: low-growing bushy shrub, 3-10' (.9-3 m) wide, of oval or egg-shaped, segmented flat stems

Stem: multiple light green stem segments (pads), turning purple in winter; each fuzzy pad, 5-8" (13-20 cm) long and 3-4" (7.5-10 cm) wide, is firmly attached

Spines: usually spineless; when present, reddish brown with yellow tips; up to 2" (5 cm) long

Spine Clusters: diagonal rows of 5-7 slightly raised, round areas (areoles) across the pad; each areole packed with dense circles of hair-like, reddish or yellowish brown spines (glochids) radiating outward; sometimes each areole has 1-3 spines that point downward

Flower: red or golden yellow blossoms on upper edges of pads; each cup-shaped flower, 2-3" (5-7.5 cm) wide, has a center of pale yellow, pink and green flower parts; sometimes inner petals of yellow flowers are orange or red

Blooming: April-May

Fruit: pear-shaped fleshy green pod, 1⅜" (3.5 cm) long, turning red when ripe; spineless, but with many prickly glochids; contains juicy pulp

Habitat: rangelands between 325-650' (100-200 m); on dry gravelly hillsides

Range: southwestern Texas along the Rio Grande near Laredo

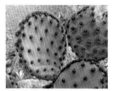

Chenille Prickly Pear
rings of long, dense
glochids

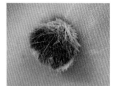

Blind Prickly Pear *(pg. 287)*
dense tuft of short
glochids

Blind Prickly Pear *(pg. 287)*
flowers are always yellow
or orange, not red

Compare: The spineless round pads of Blind Prickly Pear (pg. 287) look similar to Chenille Prickly Pear, but Blind has tufts of very short, hair-like, reddish brown spines (glochids), while Chenille has oval pads with dense circles of longer glochids and sometimes a few spines. Chenille flowers can be red or yellow, while Blind flowers are never red.

Notes: An unusual, small prickly pear with rings of fairly long, reddish brown glochids covering its fuzzy pads. Also commonly called Cowboy's Red Whiskers. Close-up photographs of circular areas (areoles) have been likened to dirty snowballs stuck all over with reddish yellow daggers. Newly sprouted pads and flower buds have glochids and temporary conical leaves.

Handle the pads carefully! Glochids readily detach from the plant, and a slight brush against them embeds many nearly invisible barbed spines into skin, where they are hard to see and remove. Embedded glochids impart a burning, prickly sensation. Remove from skin by placing sticky tape on the affected site and pulling up.

Limited in the wild to a small area of Texas in the United States, but also found across the Rio Grande in Tamaulipas and Nuevo León, Mexico. The spineless form with red blossoms is widely cultivated as an ornamental, even as far away as Australia and Europe.

glochids

flower

fruit

e page 357 for
larger map

Blind Prickly Pear
Opuntia rufida

Size: H 2-6' (.6-1.8 m)

Shape: upright, densely branching, wide shrub, 3-10' (.9-3 m) wide, of many segmented flat stems that are round, elliptical or kidney-shaped; sometimes with a short wide trunk

Stem: multiple pale yellowish green stem segments (pads) with reddish brown spots; each spineless pad, 4-8" (10-20 cm) long and 2-10" (5-25 cm) wide, is covered with tiny soft hairs; pads can turn red in cold weather

Spines: spineless

Spine Clusters: diagonal rows of 8-13 closely spaced, circular areas (areoles) across each pad; each areole is packed with grayish white wool and dense tufts of hair-like, reddish brown-to-gray spines (glochids)

Flower: golden yellow blossoms on upper edges of pads, turning orange with age; each cup-shaped flower, 2-3" (5-7.5 cm) wide, has many glossy petals with red bases around a yellow and dark green center

Blooming: April-May

Fruit: barrel-shaped fleshy green pod, 1" (2.5 cm) long, turning pinkish red when ripe, smooth surface is spotted with glochids, pale green pulp inside contains yellowish tan seeds

wide, scaly trunk

Habitat: deserts from 1,800-4,000' (550-1,220 m); flats, hillsides, canyons; volcanic, limestone, sandy or gravelly soils

Range: far western Texas along the border with Mexico, especially along the Rio Grande

Blind Prickly Pear
spineless pads have dense
glochids, many areoles

Chenille Prickly Pear
(pg. 283)
fewer areoles,
short spines

Western Prickly Pear
(pg. 255)
a few spines remain,
widely spaced areoles

Compare: Pads of the very similar Chenille Prickly Pear (pg. 283) can have short yellow spines and have fewer circular areas (areoles) than the spineless pads of Blind Prickly Pear. Western Prickly Pear (pg. 255) pads can be mostly spineless, but a few short white spines usually remain in the areoles on upper edges of the pads. Western has fewer and more widely spaced areoles than does Blind.

Notes: The only cactus in Texas in the *Opuntia* genus that has a velvety covering of tiny soft hairs on the skin of the pads. Also has dense tufts of hair-like spines (glochids), which can be dislodged by grazing cattle. The glochids can cause blindness if they get into their eyes, giving rise to another common name, Cow Blinder.

The species name *rufida* means "red," for the rust-colored glochids in each areole. Also, the color of the pads can turn red in cold weather. Sometimes called Cinnamon Prickly Pear.

One of two native spineless prickly pear species in Texas, Blind Prickly Pear is most common in northern Mexico and ranges across the border only near the Rio Grande. Found nowhere else in the United States.

spines

flower

immature fruit

See page 357 for larger map

SEGMENTED

Prickly Pear

Spinyfruit Prickly Pear
Opuntia spinosibacca

Size: H 3¼-5' (1-1.5 m)

Shape: upright shrub, branching into oval or egg-shaped, flattened segmented stems

Stem: multiple yellowish or pale green stem segments (pads) with a purple spot near each spine cluster; each pad, 4-10" (10-25 cm) long and 3-4½" (7.5-11 cm) wide, is firmly attached and has shallow bumps called tubercles (unusual in prickly pears) tipped with spine clusters

Spines: white with red bases, or reddish brown to black with lighter tips; 1-3" (2.5-7.5 cm) long; aging to gray

Spine Clusters: diagonal rows of 4-5 widely spaced clusters; circular areas (areoles) with gray wool, 1-8 spreading central spines and 2 smaller paler radial spines; areoles near the base of pad may lack spines; dense, hair-like, yellow-to-brown spines (glochids) in tufts above and surrounding each cluster

Flower: golden yellow and red blooms on spiny green flower stems atop the upper edges of pads; each bloom, 2-3" (5-7.5 cm) wide, has broad, spoon-shaped petals with red bases and midveins; light yellow, cream and yellowish green flower parts

Blooming: April-May

Fruit: oval or flat-topped conical pod, 1¼" (3 cm) long, dotted with areoles with 1-4 reddish brown and white spines; turns yellow or red, then dries out; usually sterile, sometimes with few tan seeds

spiny green
flower stalk

Habitat: deserts between 1,600-3,000' (490-915 m); limestone hillsides, canyons

Range: small area in the Big Bend region of far western Texas

Brown-spine Prickly Pear *(pg. 263)*
sprawling or creeping plants, pads touch the ground

Comanche Prickly Pear
spines limited to upper parts of pad

Sweet Prickly Pear
shorter spines across most of pad

Compare: Once thought to be a variety of the sprawling or creeping Brown-spine Prickly Pear (pg. 263), Spinyfruit Prickly Pear is more upright, with its pads held up off the ground. The variety of Brown-spine called Comanche Prickly Pear has spines only on the upper parts of its pads, differing from the spine clusters of Spinyfruit, which cover nearly the entire pad. Sweet Prickly Pear (another variety of Brown-spine) has spines across most of the pad, but the spines are fewer and shorter than those of Spinyfruit.

Notes: Genetic studies have determined that Spinyfruit Prickly Pear is a hybrid plant, the result of pollination between species. One of Spinyfruit's parent species is probably Big Bend Prickly Pear (pg. 271), which has all-reddish purple pads and from which the purple splotches on Spinyfruit pads may have been inherited. The other parent could be one of two varieties of Brown-spine Prickly Pear—the upright variety found in Big Bend called Comanche Prickly Pear or the one called Sweet Prickly Pear.

The species name *spinosibacca* is derived from the Latin words *spina* for "spine" and *bacca* for "berry." Spinyfruit is found only on limestone slopes in the hottest, driest parts of Big Bend National Park. Evidence of ancient seas, limestone is formed from the calcium-rich bodies of tiny plankton laid down in layers on the ocean floor.

spines

flower

fruit

e page 357 for
larger map

Prickly Pear

Coastal Prickly Pear
Opuntia stricta

Size: H 2-6½' (.6-2 m)

Shape: upright or sprawling shrub of narrowly elliptical or egg-shaped, flat segmented stems; sometimes has a short cylindrical trunk

Stem: multiple dull or grayish green stem segments (pads); each pad, 4-10" (10-25 cm) long and 3-6" (7.5-15 cm) wide, has scalloped edges

Spines: spineless or when present, yellow; ½-2" (1-5 cm) long; aging to brown

Spine Clusters: diagonal rows of 3-5 circular areas (areoles) are spineless or with 1-11 straight or curving, spreading spines per cluster; spines in most areoles across pad or only in upper margins of pads; each cluster has brown wool and inconspicuous crescents of hair-like, yellow-to-brown spines (glochids)

Flower: all-yellow blossoms on the upper edges of pads; each widely cup-shaped flower, 2-3" (5-7.5 cm) wide, with broad rounded petals around a wide center of yellow flower parts

Blooming: February-July

Fruit: spineless, fleshy, barrel-shaped pod, 1½-2½" (4-6 cm) long, turning red when ripe; contains juicy, purplish red pulp with tan seeds

Habitat: coastal areas at sea level; hummocks, sand dunes, open areas
Range: small area in southeastern Texas along the coast

Coastal Prickly Pear
yellow spines on flat pads

Eastern Prickly Pear
(pg. 259)
white or brown spines

Cockspur Prickly Pear
(pg. 239)
thicker, smaller pads

Compare: Coastal Prickly Pear is easily confused with Eastern Prickly Pear (pg. 259), which is widespread across the eastern United States. Both species can be spineless. When spines are present on Coastal pads, they are yellow, not white or brown as in Eastern. Cockspur Prickly Pear (pg. 239), which also can be found in southeastern Texas on coastal sand dunes, has thicker, smaller pads than Coastal.

Notes: Coastal Prickly Pear hybridizes frequently with Engelmann Prickly Pear (pg. 299) in southeastern Texas and in Louisiana, forming a yellow-spined, tree-like cactus that can grow as tall as 10 feet (3 m). Also native to Central and South America, Mexico, Bermuda and West Indies.

This prickly pear became an invasive weed after being introduced to South Africa and Australia to grow for cattle fodder and as food for cochineal insects, from which an acid is extracted to produce a red dye. It has invaded and formed dense infestations over large areas of Kruger National Park in South Africa, partly due to elephants, which eat the fruit and pads and disseminate the seeds. Once called the worst weed in Australia, burying 60 million acres (24 million ha) in the state of Queensland under dense mats as deep as 6½ feet (2 m). Introduction of South American Cactus Moths has been successful in controlling this weed in many areas of Australia. Ironically, cochineal insects have also been used to eradicate this prickly pear.

yellow spines

white spines

fruit

ee page 357 for
larger map

Engelmann Prickly Pear
Opuntia engelmannii

Size: H 3-10' (.9-3 m)

Shape: shrubby, mostly trunkless cactus of tall spreading clumps, 6-15' (1.8-4.6 m) wide, with large flat segmented stems

Stem: multiple dull yellowish green or bluish green stem segments (pads); each pad, 6-12" (15-30 cm) long and 5-10" (13-25 cm) wide, is oval or circular with straight or slightly curved spines; the pads are firmly attached

Spines: all yellow or chalky white, sometimes with dark reddish brown bases; ¹/₂-3" (1-7.5 cm) long; spines turn black with age

Spine Clusters: diagonal rows of 5-8 clusters widely spaced across the pad; 1-6 spines per cluster, 3-5 longer spines pointing or bent abruptly downward; hair-like, yellow-to-reddish brown spines (glochids) in irregular tufts surround each cluster

Flower: many buttery yellow flowers, turning apricot with age, on the upper edges of pads; each cup-shaped bloom, 2-3" (5-7.5 cm) wide, has layers of petals around pale yellow and green flower parts; plants in southern Texas can produce orange, pink, red or yellow flowers

Blooming: mid-April through May, over several weeks

Fruit: barrel-shaped spineless green pod, 1-3" (2-7.5 cm) long, turning dark red when ripe with juicy, edible, dark red pulp containing flat tan seeds

new pad

Habitat: desert plains, thorn scrub, grasslands and woodlands up to 6,000' (1,830 m); ridges, slopes, flats, along washes, valleys, canyons; sandy to gravelly soils

Range: western, central and southern Texas

Engelmann Prickly Pear
short, pale yellow or white spines and many glochids

Brown-spine Prickly Pear (pg. 263)
longer, brown and white spines

Chisos Mountain Prickly Pear (pg. 303)
longer, dark yellow spines and fewer glochids

Compare: Much like Brown-spine Prickly Pear (pg. 263), with which it hybridizes. Engelmann Prickly Pear spines are short and pale yellow or white, not like the longer reddish brown or brown and white spines of Brown-spine. Chisos Mountain Prickly Pear (pg. 303) has longer spines and fewer glochids than Engelmann.

Notes: The most abundant and conspicuous cactus in Texas. Common across the Southwest and northern Mexico. Recognizable by its large pads, short spines (yellow or white) and widely spreading, tall form. Sometimes has a short central woody stem.

Two main varieties of Engelmann Prickly Pear grow in Texas. The yellow-spined type, commonly known as Texas Prickly Pear (*O. engelmannii* var. *lindheimeri*), is more widespread and found mostly east of the Pecos River. A white-spined variety grows west of the Pecos River in far western Texas. Although this species usually has all-yellow blooms, Texas Prickly Pear plants growing in southern Texas can have blossoms that are orange, pink or red.

New lime green pads with tiny conical leaves face east and west for longer exposure to the sun during monsoon season. These young spineless pads can be cooked as a vegetable. Also called Cactus Apple for its fruit, from which juice and jams are made. Pack rats eat the fruit and build nest mounds in the midst of Engelmann clumps, using the spiny pads to form a protective barrier.

301

spines

flower

fruit

ee page 358 for
larger map

Chisos Mountain Prickly Pear
Opuntia chisosensis

Size: H 3-10' (.9-3 m), but usually 3' (.9 m)

Shape: upright medium-sized shrub, 6' (1.8 m) wide, branching from a thick base, with flat segmented stems

Stem: up to 6 grayish green or bluish green stem segments (pads) per branch; each oval or circular pad, 6-12" (15-30 cm) long and 5-10" (13-25 cm) wide, has spines on the upper third; pads are firmly attached

Spines: bright yellow with pale yellow tips; spines turn reddish orange, then black with age; 1¼-2½" (3-6 cm) long

Spine Clusters: diagonal rows of 4-7 clusters widely spaced across the pad; 1-5 spines per cluster with 1 longest spine curving downward; a few hair-like yellow spines (glochids) form a crescent over some clusters

Flower: pale yellow flowers, turning orangish yellow with age, on the upper edges of pads; each cup-shaped bloom, 2-2½" (5-6 cm) wide, has petals with wavy blunt edges around yellow and green flower parts

Blooming: May-early June, over a period of several weeks

Fruit: conical green pod, 1-1½" (2.5-4 cm) long, has yellow bristles at top; turns bright red when ripe with sweet, edible, beet red pulp that is juicy and contains yellow seeds

Habitat: meadows, oak/pine/juniper woodlands from 5,200-7,200′ (1,585-2,195 m); canyons, grassy slopes

Range: only in the Chisos Mountains in far western Texas

**Chisos Mountain
Prickly Pear**
has yellow spines

Engelmann Prickly Pear
(pg. 299)
white or yellow spines
or spineless

Engelmann Prickly Pear
(pg. 299)
dark red fruit

Compare: The yellow-spined variety of Engelmann Prickly Pear (pg. 299) is very similar to Chisos Mountain Prickly Pear, but has dark red, not bright red fruit.

Notes: Prickly pear cacti are noted for the difficulty in identifying them and for causing many disagreements on how to classify them into species. A medium-sized shrub with upright branches, long yellow spines and buff-to-pale yellow flowers, Chisos Mountain Prickly Pear was once considered to be a variety of Engelmann Prickly Pear. On the basis of genetic studies, it is now thought to be more closely related to Big Bend Prickly Pear (pg. 271), which usually has reddish purple or purplish green pads.

The range of this cactus is thought to be limited in the United States to the Chisos Mountains of Brewster County, Texas. The Chisos Mountain range is contained entirely within Big Bend National Park, 800,000 acres (320,000 ha) bordering Mexico and containing the largest protected area of the Chihuahuan Desert in the United States. Some cactus enthusiasts think that yellow-spined prickly pears found infrequently in the Davis, Guadalupe or Franklin Mountain ranges of far western Texas may belong to this species, but other experts disagree. Chisos Mountain Prickly Pear is also found in Mexico.

spines

flower

fruit

Common Dog Cholla
Grusonia schottii

ee page 358 for larger map

Size: H 3-3½" (7.5-9 cm)

Shape: spreading mats, up to 17' (5.2 m) wide, branching near the ground into chains of segmented stems

Stem: multiple green stem segments (joints), each 1⅜-2½" (3.5-6 cm) long and ¾-1¼" (2-3 cm) wide, club-shaped with long conspicuous knobs (tubercles) and spines; the spines do little to hide the stem color; segments fall off readily

Spines: white, yellow, tan, and bright reddish brown to dull pinkish brown; 1¼-2¾" (3-7 cm) long; aging to gray

Spine Clusters: dense interlacing clusters; each circular area (areole) packed with grayish white wool and 11-17 stout spines of varying lengths pointing in different directions; some spines are flattened; hair-like yellow spines (glochids) in sparse tufts at the top of each cluster

Flower: bright yellow flowers clustered at the tips of stems; each bloom, 1-2" (2.5-5 cm) wide, has slightly cupped petals with male flower parts (stamens) made up of green filaments and yellow anthers, and a cream-colored female flower part (stigma)

Blooming: May-early July; opens midday, closes late afternoon

Fruit: cylindrical yellow fruit, 1-2" (2.5-5 cm) long, dotted with tufts of yellow or white glochids, white wool and few short spines; fleshy, containing pale seeds

Habitat: desert scrub and thorn scrub between 100-4,000' (30-1,220 m); flats, hills; limestone or volcanic, gravelly or sandy soils deposited by running water

Range: western and southern Texas, and a couple of isolated areas in the central part of the state

Common Dog Cholla
major central spines are
reddish brown

Clumped Dog Cholla
(pg. 311)
spines are grayish white

Clumped Dog Cholla
(pg. 311)
red and yellow stamens,
not green and yellow

Compare: Common Dog Cholla resembles Clumped Dog Cholla (pg. 311), but Clumped has grayish white spines, not the bright reddish brown or dull pinkish brown central spines of Common. The male flower parts (stamens) of Clumped flowers often have red filaments, while Common filaments are green.

Notes: There are eight species of dog cholla in the Southwest, four of which are seen in Texas. This aptly named species is the most common and conspicuous dog cholla in the state. Grows only in the Chihuahuan Desert and in Tamaulipan thorn scrub of Texas and Mexico.

Dog chollas are easily recognized by the way they branch near the ground and form creeping mats. They differ only in segment size, spine cluster pattern, flower color and number of spines on the fruit. The club-shaped stem segments are narrow at the base and thicker on top, with noticeable knobs (tubercles). The hollow, woody, net-like skeletons of dead plants resemble those of the taller chollas in the *Cylindropuntia* genus.

The spiny stem segments of this dog cholla detach so easily that they are accused of "reaching out to touch someone." Spines have tiny fishhook-like barbs, so what goes into flesh or clothing doesn't come out easily. Experienced desert hikers learn to carry a comb to brush the spiny stems off themselves and their pets. Some dislike dog chollas since they can become embedded in shoes or boots.

spines

immature fruit

e page 358 for
larger map

SEGMENTED

Dog Cholla

Clumped Dog Cholla
Grusonia aggeria

Size: H 1-6" (2.5-15 cm)

Shape: short spreading mats, up to 3' (.9 m) wide, branching near the ground into chains of segmented stems

Stem: multiple green or reddish green stem segments (joints), each 1-3½" (2.5-9 cm) long and ⅝-1¼" (1.5-3 cm) wide, club-shaped with conspicuous knobs (tubercles); segments not easily detached

Spines: mostly grayish white (younger spines with pinkish brown bases), some central spines purplish brown to black; 1¼-2" (3-5 cm) long

Spine Clusters: each cluster has circular areas (areoles) packed with white wool and 5-15 formidable spines of varying lengths; 3-4 stout central spines point in all directions, some are flattened; slender radial spines are bent downward; numerous hair-like yellow spines (glochids) in large tufts at the top of many clusters

Flower: bright yellow flowers clustered at the tips of stems; each bloom, 1½-2" (4-5 cm) wide, has 3-4 layers of slightly cupped petals with red and yellow male flower parts (stamens) and a pale green-to-creamy yellow female flower part (stigma); outer petals sometimes are red

Blooming: late March-April; opening about midday, closing in late afternoon

Fruit: fleshy cylindrical green fruit, 1-2" (2.5-5 cm) long, dotted with white wool, tufts of yellow glochids and few short spines; ripening to pale yellow and becoming gray and dry with age

SEGMENTED STEMS; **Dog Cholla** 311

Habitat: deserts from 1,800-3,500' (550-1,065 m); flats, hills, among creosote bushes; gravelly or silty soils deposited by running water and made of limestone, volcanic or gypsum rock

Range: restricted to the Big Bend area of far western Texas

Clumped Dog Cholla
most spines are
grayish white

Big Bend Dog Cholla
(pg. 315)
spines are longer and
pinkish tan

Common Dog Cholla
(pg. 307)
stem segments fall
off readily

Compare: Clumped Dog Cholla resembles Big Bend Dog Cholla (pg. 315), but Big Bend has nine longer, pinkish tan central spines, while Clumped has 3-4 grayish white central spines. Common Dog Cholla (pg. 307) stem segments fall off easily, while Clumped stem segments do not.

Notes: Most common within 20 miles (32 km) of the Rio Grande, this low-growing dog cholla is found only in Presidio and Brewster counties of far western Texas and south into Mexico. The species name *aggeria* is from the Latin word for "mound" and refers to the short, spreading, mounded mats formed by this cactus. Usually very spiny, some plants have only a few short spines and appear nearly spineless.

Dog chollas are closely related to the large cacti in the genus *Cylindropuntia*, but are sprawling and have club-shaped branches rather than upright cylindrical branches like those of the large chollas. Unlike other dog chollas, which have stems that easily detach, Clumped segments cling stubbornly to the stems and are one way to distinguish it from similar species.

Clumped Dog Cholla is often confusingly referred to as Big Bend Prickly Pear, but it is not the Big Bend Prickly Pear on pg. 271. However, the related prickly pear cacti usually have paddle-shaped flat stem segments.

spines

immature fruit

see page 358 for larger map

SEGMENTED

Dog Cholla

Big Bend Dog Cholla
Grusonia densispina

Size: H 3-5" (7.5-13 cm)

Shape: compact spreading mats, up to 10' (3 m) wide, branching near the ground into short chains of sprawling segmented stems

Stem: multiple stem segments (joints), each 1¾-2¾" (4.5-7 cm) long and 1⅜" (3.5 cm) wide, oblong to club-shaped with conspicuous knobs (tubercles) mostly obscured by dense spines; segments are securely attached

Spines: white, pinkish white or tan; 1-3" (2.5-7.5 cm) long

Spine Clusters: each cluster has 9 long flattened central spines, twisted and curved and pointing in all directions; 2-4 slender radial spines bent downward; numerous long, hair-like yellow spines (glochids) in large tufts at the top of many clusters

Flower: bright yellow flowers clustered at the tips of stems; each bloom, 1½-2" (4-5 cm) wide, has slightly cupped petals, all-yellow or red and yellow male flower parts (stamens) and a pale green-to-creamy yellow female flower part (stigma); outer petal tips sometimes tinged red

Blooming: mid-May through early June; opening midday, closing late afternoon

Fruit: fleshy club-shaped green fruit, 1-2" (2.5-5 cm) long, dotted with white wool and tufts of tan glochids; fruit ripens to lemon yellow, then turns brown and dry with age

SEGMENTED STEMS; **Dog Cholla** 315

Habitat: deserts between 2,000-2,200' (610-670 m); flats; clay soils or gravel over clay

Range: restricted to near the Rio Grande in Big Bend National Park in far western Texas

Big Bend Dog Cholla
more numerous spines
are longer

Common Dog Cholla
(pg. 307)
flower usually has green,
not red, filaments

Common Dog Cholla
(pg. 307)
stem segments are
easily detached

Compare: Big Bend Dog Cholla has more numerous and longer spines than the very similar Common Dog Cholla (pg. 307). The flowers of Common have green and yellow stamens, not all yellow or red and yellow like the blooms of Big Bend. Also unlike Common, its stem segments are securely attached and do not readily brush off.

Notes: A low-growing, mounding cactus with segmented, club-shaped branches that have long spines. Blooms in May and June, the hottest months in the Chihuahuan Desert. Sometimes considered a variety of the closely related Common Dog Cholla rather than a separate species. Those botanists who believe this is a separate species point to the longer denser spines and larger overall appearance of Big Bend Dog Cholla.

Although very limited in distribution, it is possible for many to see this very spiny cactus along River Road near Solis Ranch in Big Bend National Park. This unique preserve has a wide variety of habitats, ranging from hot parched deserts to cool moist forests of fir and aspen in the mountains. It contains over 1,200 plant species (about 60 are cacti). Some cacti are found only in this region in the U.S., but also grow in Mexico. A few cactus species, including Big Bend Dog Cholla, occur only in Big Bend National Park and nowhere else in the world. The ranges of many eastern, western and Mexican plant and animal species overlap there, and it is famous for having more species of cacti, birds and bats than any other U.S. national park.

spines

flower

fruit

see page 358 for larger map

Icicle Cholla
Cylindropuntia tunicata

Size: H 12-24" (30-61 cm)

Shape: low-growing, widely spreading clumps or mats, 2-6' (.6-1.8 m) wide, of 50 or more short segmented stems

Stem: multiple pale green stem segments (joints), each 2-8" (5-20 cm) long and ⅝-1" (1.5-2.5 cm) wide, with broad prominent bumps (tubercles) and spines totally hiding the green stems; segments detach easily

Spines: translucent, tan spines; 1-2½" (2.5-6 cm) long

Spine Clusters: overlapping clusters; 5-12 stout long sharp spines per cluster pointing in all directions; hair-like, pale yellow spines (glochids) in a small tuft below the spine cluster

Flower: several yellowish green flowers at the tips of stems; each flower, 1⅜-2" (3.5-5 cm) wide, has 1 layer of petals with green midstripes, around orangish yellow and green flower parts

Blooming: May-July, over a period of several weeks

Fruit: yellow pod, ⅔-1" (1.6-2.5 cm) long, is broadly cone-shaped, spineless, with very knobby tubercles; fleshy, containing tan seeds; ripens 2 months after blooming and stays on the cactus throughout the winter

Habitat: grasslands and juniper woodlands between 4,500-5,000' (1,370-1,525 m); south-facing rocky limestone slopes

Range: limited to two counties in far western Texas

Icicle Cholla
yellowish green flower
with yellow stamens

Thistle Cholla *(pg. 323)*
greenish yellow flower
with red and yellow
stamens

Big Bend Dog Cholla
(pg. 315)
resembles small mats of
Icicle Cholla

Compare: Resembles the closely related Thistle Cholla (pg. 323), which has bronze-tinged, greenish yellow blooms with male flower parts (stamens) made up of red filaments and yellow anthers, not mostly green flowers with all-yellow stamens like Icicle Cholla. Small clumps of Icicle Cholla look like some dog chollas, such as Big Bend Dog Cholla (pg. 315), but the spines of Icicle Cholla are all yellow.

Notes: A formidable-looking cactus with translucent pale yellow spines covering a short dense mass of stems that branch upright from a woody, creeping stem. When backlit with early morning or late afternoon light, the spines glow as though lit from within, giving them a silvery white, ice-coated appearance–thus the common name. "Icicle" may also refer to the thick, pointed shape of the spines. This cholla also spreads by its stem segments, which drop off readily, littering the ground around the plant. The segments sprout roots and grow into new plants.

Found only in two counties in far western Texas–in Pecos County on south-facing limestone slopes and in two secret sites in Brewster County. Seen along the west side of Highway 385, where the highway enters the southern part of the Glass Mountain range. More widespread in Mexico and in Chile, Ecuador and Argentina in South America, where it is called Abrojo. Also an invasive weed in western Australia. Historically, the roots were used as a laxative.

spines

flower

fruit

Thistle Cholla
Cylindropuntia davisii

e page 358 for
larger map

Size: H 8-34" (20-86 cm)

Shape: short upright cactus, branching many times from the slender woody trunk and again along the divided cylindrical stems; spines often obscure the branches

Stem: multiple light green stem segments (joints), each 2½-5" (6-13 cm) long and ½" (1 cm) wide, with prominent slender bumps (tubercles) and long spines covering up the skin color; outer segments easily detach

Spines: yellowish brown or reddish brown to nearly black or gray with yellow tips; ⅝-2" (1.5-5 cm) long

Spine Clusters: overlapping clusters; each cluster has 7-13 spines (some flattened) of unequal length pointing in all directions; gray or yellow wool and a tuft of hair-like yellow spines (glochids) below each cluster

Flower: waxy-looking, greenish yellow flowers atop spiny, cone-shaped stalks at the tips of stems; each wide-open, cup-shaped blossom, 1½" (4 cm) wide, has overlapping petals with bronze-tinged tips around red and yellow flower parts

Blooming: June-July; opening midday, closing at night, lasting only 1 day

Fruit: teardrop-shaped yellow pod, 1-1⅜" (2.5-3.5 cm) long, slightly fleshy with tubercles; rarely containing few pale yellow seeds; ripens in September

Habitat: mountain valleys, grasslands and oak/juniper/mesquite woodlands between 3,500-5,000' (1,065-1,525 m); plains, slopes; soils deposited by rivers or other running water

Range: scattered areas in far western, central and northwestern Texas

Thistle Cholla
some reddish
brown spines

Icicle Cholla *(pg. 319)*
all-yellow spines

Icicle Cholla *(pg. 319)*
lower-growing,
denser mound

Compare: Resembles the closely related Icicle Cholla (pg. 319), which differs by having all-yellow spines, as compared to some reddish brown spines of Thistle Cholla. Icicle Cholla grows in low dense mounds, not as upright plants like Thistle Cholla.

Notes: Although widespread in western Texas, this small cholla is scattered and uncommon, usually occurring as a solitary plant. Fairly tolerant of cold, it is also found in the wild in southeastern Oklahoma and northern New Mexico.

When Thistle Cholla is actively growing, it produces slim conical leaves on the new stem segments. These leaves are temporary and replaced later by spines. Spines vary in color from pale yellow to dark brown and are so long and dense that they mostly obscure the branching stems. This cactus can be overlooked, mistaken for a large dried grass clump or mound from a distance.

Very often the flowers are not fertilized, and the resulting fruit does not contain seeds. Usually seen growing as solitary plants. Sometimes reproduces by rooting from fallen stem segments, forming small colonies of less than a dozen plants. Unlike most other chollas, only the outer stem segments of Thistle Cholla detach easily.

spines

flower

fruit

ee page 359 for larger map

SEGMENTED

Cholla

Desert Christmas Cholla
Cylindropuntia leptocaulis

Size: H 2-6' (.6-1.8 m)

Shape: compact shrubby or upright straggly cactus with many extremely thin, branching segmented stems

Stem: many stem segments (joints), yellowish green or grayish green, each 1-3" (2.5-7.5 cm) long and ¹⁄₅-¹⁄₄" (.5-.6 cm) wide, with few to many spines and long, narrow, closely spaced ridges (tubercles) that are smooth and nearly inconspicuous after rain, but wrinkled in drought; loosely attached segments

Spines: gray with yellow tips or white with golden brown ends; ¹⁄₄-1³⁄₄" (.6-4.5 cm) long

Spine Clusters: 1 spine (rarely 3) in each round area (areole) along the stems and pointing straight out; outer segments and some whole plants are spineless with hair-like, yellowish brown spines (glochids) in a tuft near or encircling each areole

Flower: 1 to several delicate pale yellow flowers alternating along the outer stems; each bloom, ¹⁄₂-1" (1-2.5 cm) wide, has backward-curving petals with red-tinged tips; many upright, pale yellow flower parts

Blooming: June-August, over a period of several weeks; opening in the afternoon and closing sometime after dark, lasting just 1 day

Fruit: grape-shaped, smooth-skinned, yellowish green pod, ³⁄₄" (2 cm) long; spineless, but with tufts of glochids; fleshy, edible, turning scarlet red or bright yellow when ripe with tiny pale yellow seeds; ripens 5 months after flowering and stays on the plant throughout winter

Habitat: desert scrub, thorn scrub, grasslands and woodlands up to 5,000' (1,525 m); flats, along washes, slopes, canyons, among other low shrubs, under trees

Range: throughout most of Texas, but especially the western two-thirds of the state

Desert Christmas Cholla
each spine cluster has
1 central spine pointing
straight out or down

Tree Cholla (pg. 331)
thicker stem, more and
shorter spines

Klein Cholla
hybrid has spinier,
thicker stem

Compare: With widths of less than ¼ inch (.6 cm), Desert Christmas Cholla branches are the slimmest of any cactus, so this plant is not easily confused with other chollas in Texas. Other Texas chollas, such as Tree Cholla (pg. 331), have thick stems and many more spines. Desert Christmas hybridizes with Tree Cholla and results in a spinier, thicker-stemmed plant called Klein Cholla.

Notes: Desert Christmas Cholla is the most widespread of the cholla cacti. Its range covers about two-thirds of Texas, three-quarters of Arizona, half of New Mexico, the Arbuckle Mountains of Oklahoma and much of northern Mexico. In far western Texas, this cholla will hybridize with Tree Cholla, producing a plant called Klein Cholla. When taller plants are present, Desert Christmas is always found growing beneath a desert tree or bush. The stems can become as long as 15 feet (4.6 m) when growing up through and supported by a tall mesquite tree.

The edible fruit is relished by birds and other desert creatures, and was eaten by American Indians. The scarlet red color of the fruit stands out from the dull gray and tan hues of the desert in winter. "Christmas" in the common name refers to the time of year when the fruit ripens and perhaps to its festive appearance. In southern Texas, some of the ripe fruit is bright yellow.

spines

flower

fruit

Tree Cholla
Cylindropuntia imbricata

ee page 359 for
larger map

Size: H 3-10' (.9-3 m)

Shape: large shrub or small tree with a short trunk and many-branched, cylindrical segmented stems that are upright or drooping

Stem: multiple grayish green stem segments (joints); each joint, 4-16" (10-40 cm) long and ⅝-1½" (1.5-4 cm) wide, with large bumpy protuberances (tubercles) partially covered by the spines; stems do not easily detach

Spines: silvery white, or grayish white-to-tan-to-yellow spines; ⅓-1½" (.8-4 cm) long

Spine Clusters: 8-15 stout, straight or slightly curved spines per cluster; dense tuft of bristle-like yellow spines (glochids) below each cluster; some round areas (areoles) are spineless

Flower: several pink-to-magenta-to-red flowers at the tips of stems; each cup-shaped bloom, 1-3" (2.5-7.5 cm) wide, has a couple layers of petals that are darker at their bases, around a center of yellow and pink flower parts

Blooming: May-June, over a period of several weeks

Fruit: broadly cone-shaped, bright yellow pod, 1-2" (2.5-5 cm) long, spineless with very prominent tubercles, fleshy, containing yellowish tan seeds

skeleton

Habitat: deserts, juniper woodlands, grasslands and mountains from 2,000-7,300' (610-2,225 m); flats, rocky limestone slopes, ridges, canyons, along washes; among other succulent plants such as lechuguillas and sotols

Range: far western, west central and northwestern Texas

Tree Cholla
shorter spines,
pink flowers

Thistle Cholla *(pg. 323)*
longer spines

Thistle Cholla *(pg. 323)*
greenish yellow flower

Compare: The related Thistle Cholla (pg. 323) has longer spines in its closely spaced clusters, so it appears much spinier than Tree Cholla. Thistle Cholla flower petals are greenish yellow, rather than some shade of pink like Tree Cholla blossoms. Thistle Cholla is much less common than Tree Cholla.

Notes: An abundant cactus in the Chihuahuan Desert. Often grows out in the open surrounded by brown grasses or rocks that make it stand out as the only green plant around. After the plant dies, the long branches dry to reveal a hollow skeletal cane that can be used as a walking stick, thus another name, Walkingstick Cholla.

Stout long spines covering the green stems in one variety of this species give the plant a fuzzy, straw-colored appearance from afar. In another type where the shorter spines don't hide the stem, the vivid lemon yellow fruit contrasts sharply with the dull green stem color.

The upper portion of the round areas (areoles) sometimes contain yellow or gray bumps that secrete sweet liquid droplets that ants feed upon–an instance of a plant structure other than a flower having nectar. Presumably in return, the ants patrol the cactus and prevent other insects from eating the stems.

Grows at higher elevations and can tolerate colder temperatures than the other chollas found in Texas. Also found in Colorado, New Mexico and Mexico, and is spreading into Oklahoma and Kansas.

spines

flower

fruit

Cereus

Desert Night-blooming Cereus
Peniocereus greggii

e page 359 for
larger map

Size: H 1½-6½' (.5-2 m)

Shape: upright or sprawling cactus with long, slender, sometimes branching stems

Stem: 1 to a few grayish green-to-purplish brown stems, 1⅓-4' (40-122 cm) long; each woody hollow angular stem, ½-1" (1-2.5 cm) wide, has velvety skin and 4-6 ribs lined with tiny spine clusters

Spines: yellowish white to gray to black; less than ¼" (.6 cm) long

Spine Clusters: widely spaced clusters on ribs; 11-15 tiny spines per cluster; spines point downward, pressed closely against the stem

Flower: 1 white blossom at the tips or sides of upright stems; each showy, fragrant flower, 2-3¼" (5-8 cm) wide, has long pointed petals (outer petals turn downward) around many cream flower parts

Blooming: April-May; opening at dusk and remaining open only for a single night, until soon after sunrise; plants in a population bloom over several days

Fruit: pear-shaped, bright red pod, 2½-3½" (6-9 cm) long, smooth and shiny, with sparse short spine clusters; dried flower tuft remains attached; pod turns dark brown when ripe with sweet juicy pulp containing many tiny black seeds; fruit remains on the stem for a few months

tuber

Habitat: desert scrub and grasslands between 3,500-5,000' (1,065-1,525 m); flats, bajadas, along washes, among creosote bushes, under mesquite or acacia trees; silty or sandy limestone or lava soils

Range: far western Texas

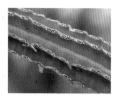

Desert Night-blooming Cereus
angular stem with 6 ribs

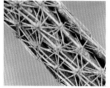

Dahlia Hedgehog *(pg. 227)*
rounded stem

Dahlia Hedgehog *(pg. 227)*
pink flower

Compare: Often mistaken for creosote bush branches. The only similar cactus in Texas is Dahlia Hedgehog (pg. 227). The pink-flowered Dahlia has 8-10 ribs on a rounded stem, not 4-6 ribs on an angular stem like Desert Night-blooming Cereus.

Notes: There are 15 species in the genus *Peniocereus* that are mainly found in Mexico, with only two occurring in the United States. Stems of this unique cactus appear dead almost year-round. Blends in with debris under branches of protective shrubs. Can grow as long as 10 feet (3 m) if supported by branches of another plant, but rarely noticed until the showy and fragrant flowers open at dusk for the night. The white glow and sweet fragrance of the blossoms attract hawk moths. The sucrose-rich nectar of a single flower provides enough energy to a hawk moth for 3-20 minutes of hovering flight. Sometimes called Queen-of-the-night for its beautiful flowers.

This cactus has a large underground tuber that can grow as big as a basketball and weigh from 15-90 pounds (6.8-41 kg). Historically, American Indians dug the tuber to use for food and treating illness.

Widespread in far western Texas, common in some areas, but rare in Big Bend National Park. Large populations of this cactus have been exterminated by collectors. Some elderly folk talk of seeing as many as 100 blossoms open on a single cactus, before collectors removed the largest plants. Propagated easily from short stem cuttings and from seed.

spines

flower

fruit

Barbed Wire Cactus

Acanthocereus tetragonus

See page 359 for larger map

Size: H 6-23' (1.8-7 m)

Shape: upright, sprawling or climbing cactus, branching at the base into long angular stems; sometimes has a trunk

Stem: multiple light-to-dark green stems; each succulent stem, 1-2" (2.5-5 cm) wide, is divided into 2-3 segments, 1-6½' (.3-2 m) long, and has 3-5 high narrow ribs lined with formidable spine clusters

Spines: light brown, sometimes with red bases; ½-1½" (1-4 cm) long, aging to gray

Spine Clusters: widely spaced clusters along ribs; each cluster has short white wool and straight or curving spines with swollen bases (1-3 longer central spines and 5-7 radial spines)

Flower: several large white blossoms along the end segments of stems; each showy, fragrant flower, 2½-5" (6-13 cm) wide, has long pointed petals around yellow and white flower parts and is supported by a long and spiny, light green flower tube

Blooming: July-September; opening near midnight and closing at dawn

Fruit: oval or oblong, bright red pod, 1-3" (2.5-7.5 cm) long, shiny with shallow bumps (tubercles) tipped with 1-4 short spines; contains sweet juicy pulp with shiny black seeds

Habitat: coastal areas below 32' (9.8 m); dense thickets, hummocks, bottomlands; moist sandy soils

Range: tip of southern Texas

Barbed Wire Cactus
succulent, angular stem

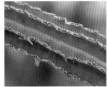

Desert Night-blooming Cereus (pg. 335)
smaller stem, appearing dead much of the year

Desert Night-blooming Cereus (pg. 335)
flower looks a lot like a Barbed Wire blossom

Compare: Desert Night-blooming Cereus (pg. 335) has angular stems like Barbed Wire Cactus, but Desert's stems are much smaller and appear brown and dead much of the year, unlike the large, succulent stems of Barbed Wire. Desert's flowers look very much like Barbed Wire blooms.

Notes: One of 12 tropical species in the *Acanthocereus* genus. Widespread, it is found mainly along the eastern coast of Mexico, ranging south to Venezuela, and on islands in the Caribbean. It is the only member of this genus occurring in the United States. Limited to the frost-free southernmost portions of Texas and Florida, it does not tolerate temperatures of 32°F (0°C) or lower.

Also called Triangle Cactus because, in the United States, most stems of mature plants are triangular with 3 narrow ribs. Young plants have 4-5 ribs. In Mexico and farther south, mature Barbed Wire can also have 4-5 ribs, thus the species name *tetragonus*.

The long, slender stems of this unique cactus grow extremely rapidly, as much as 5-6 feet (1.5-1.8 m) each summer. Stems arch over if not supported by branches of other plants, rooting at their tips where they touch the ground. The spiny, fast-growing stems are cultivated for use as barbed fences to contain livestock. Also grown throughout the Caribbean islands for its edible sweet fruit. Its large fragrant white flowers open only at night, attracting hawk moths to abundant nectar.

Glossary

Anther: A part of the male flower that contains the pollen.

Areole: The slightly raised, cushiony, usually round or oval point of attachment of cactus spines to the stem of the plant.

Arroyo: A usually dry and sandy streambed in the Southwest over which water flows during or after heavy rains. See *wash*.

Bajadas: Broad fan-like folds of sand, earth and rocks on the lower slopes of desert mountains, deposited by the erosive action of streams or washes.

Branch: A supporting part of a plant growing from the trunk or other branches and usually bearing the leaves or flowers. See *stem*.

Central spine: One of the inner, larger and longer major spines of a spine cluster, usually pointing out from the cactus stem, sometimes with a hooked tip.

Cluster: A group or collection of spines, flowers or fruit.

Creosote bush: A yellow-flowered evergreen bush with a resinous odor, most strongly fragrant after rainfall, abundant in Southwest deserts.

Desert: A barren, often sandy area of extreme temperatures, low precipitation, high rates of evaporation and sparse vegetation, as in the Chihuahuan Desert. See *desert scrub*.

Desert scrub: An area with more vegetation, such as shrubs and scattered small trees, than in deserts. See *desert*.

Ephemeral: Lasting for only a short time each spring.

Flower: To bloom, or produce a flower or flowers as a means of reproduction.

Fruit: A ripened ovary or reproductive structure that contains one or more seeds, such as a pod.

Glochid: One of the tiny, hair-like barbed spines or bristles found in tufts in the areoles of prickly pears and chollas, on stems or fruit.

Joint: A segment or section of a stem, found only in dog cholla, cholla and prickly pear cacti. See *pad*.

Lechuguilla: A succulent plant with sharply pointed, leathery leaves, found only in the Chihuahuan Desert in the Southwest and in Mexico.

Mesa: An elevated, flat expanse of land (plateau), with one or more steep sides or cliffs; Spanish for "tableland."

Novaculite: A very hard, dense rock composed mainly of microcrystalline quartz.

Nurse plant: A mature plant that shelters seedlings from the weather.

Pad: A flat, paddle-shaped stem segment of prickly pear cacti. See *joint*.

Petal: A basic flower part that is usually brightly colored, serving to attract pollinating insects.

Photosynthesis: In green plants, the conversion of water and carbon dioxide into carbohydrates (food) from energy in sunlight.

Pistil: The female part of a flower made up of an ovary, style and stigma, often in the center of the flower.

Pod: A fruit that contains many seeds, as in Tree Cholla.

Pollination: The transfer of pollen from the male anther to the female stigma, usually resulting in the production of seeds.

Radial spine: One of the outermost spines of a cluster, radiating around and spreading out from the longer, thicker central spines.

Rib: An outward vertical or wavy fold of the surface of a cactus stem, usually bearing clusters of spines.

Sepal: A member of the outermost set of petals of a flower, typically green or leafy, but often colored and resembling a petal.

Spine: A stiff, sharply pointed, woody outgrowth on a cactus.

Spine cluster: A group of spines in each areole of a cactus stem, usually including radial and central spines.

Stamen: The male parts of a flower, consisting of an anther and a filament.

Stem: An elongated supporting part of a plant growing from the root or branching from the trunk. See *branch*.

Stigma: The female part of the flower that receives the pollen.

Succulent: A plant that has thick, water-storing leaves or stems, such as in cacti.

Taproot: The primary, vertically descending root of a plant.

Thorn scrub: A subtropical, dry woodland containing short, thorny trees and shrubs that lose their leaves during drought. See *desert scrub*.

Trunk: The main stem or body of a tree or tree-like cactus, often woody and usually supporting branches.

Tubercle: A bump or projection on a cactus stem or fruit.

Tunas: The Spanish word for edible fruit of prickly pear cacti.

Wash: A usually dry and sandy streambed in the Southwest over which water flows during or after heavy rains. See *arroyo*.

Woody: Having the appearance of wood, as in stems, trunks and spines.

Wool: The long and soft, fluffy or matted hairs or fibers, similar to the coat of sheep, sometimes found on cactus fruit or in spine clusters.

Detailed Range Maps

Some Texas cactus species range over large portions of the state but others occur only in specific, localized areas. Since Texas is such a big state, it is often difficult to spot small areas on a range map. That is why we are including an enlarged range map for each species. These maps are in order of appearance in the book, and when necessary, we have magnified portions of the maps to highlight parts of the range that might otherwise be difficult to see.

Living Rock Cactus (pg. 23)

Peyote (pg. 27)

Star Cactus (pg. 31)

Golf Ball Pincushion (pg. 35)

Ping Pong Ball Cactus (pg. 39)

Button Cactus (pg. 43)

Texas Pincushion (pg. 47)

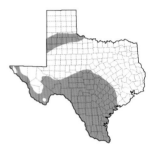

Heyder Pincushion (pg. 51)

Little Pincushion (pg. 55)

Longmamma Pincushion (pg. 59)

Rattail Pincushion (pg. 63)

Arizona Fishhook Pincushion (pg. 67)

Nellie Beehive Cactus (pg. 71)

Duncan Beehive Cactus (pg. 75)

Junior Tom Thumb Cactus (pg. 79)

Whiskerbush Beehive Cactus (pg. 83)

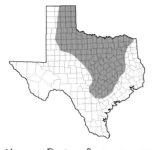

Missouri Beehive Cactus (pg. 87)

Grooved Beehive Cactus (pg. 91)

Hester Beehive Cactus (pg. 95)

Desert Beehive Cactus (pg. 99)

Lloyd Pineapple Cactus (pg. 103)

Chaffey Beehive Cactus (pg. 107)

Sea Urchin Beehive Cactus (pg. 111)

Chihuahuan Beehive Cactus (pg. 115)

Robust-spine Beehive Cactus (pg. 119)

Common Beehive Cactus (pg. 123)

Cob Beehive Cactus (pg. 127)

Warnock Pineapple Cactus (pg. 131)

Woven-spine Pineapple Cactus (pg. 135)

Big-needle Beehive Cactus (pg. 139)

Sneed Beehive Cactus (pg. 143)

Short-hook Fishhook Cactus (pg. 147)

Scheer Fishhook Cactus (pg. 151)

Chihuahuan Fishhook Cactus (pg. 155)

Twisted-rib Cactus (pg. 159)

Horse Crippler (pg. 163)

Eagle's Claw Cactus (pg. 167)

Glory-of-Texas (pg. 171)

Davis Hedgehog (pg. 175)

Lace Hedgehog (pg. 179)

Allicoche Hedgehog (pg. 183)

Fendler Hedgehog (pg. 187)

Mexican Rainbow Hedgehog (pg. 191)

Chisos Mountain Hedgehog (pg. 195)

Texas Rainbow Hedgehog (pg. 199)

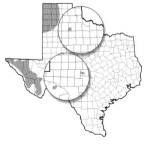

Green-flowered Hedgehog (pg. 203)

Strawberry Hedgehog (pg. 207)

Scarlet Hedgehog (pg. 211)

Pitaya (pg. 215)

Ladyfinger Hedgehog (pg. 219)

Berlandier Hedgehog (pg. 223)

Dahlia Hedgehog (pg. 227)

Turk's Head Barrel (pg. 231)

Fishhook Barrel (pg. 235)

Cockspur Prickly Pear (pg. 239)

Brittle Prickly Pear (pg. 243)

Plains Prickly Pear (pg. 247)

Potts Prickly Pear (pg. 251)

Western Prickly Pear (pg. 255)

Eastern Prickly Pear (pg. 259)

Brown-spine Prickly Pear (pg. 263)

Black-spine Prickly Pear (pg. 267)

Big Bend Prickly Pear (pg. 271)

Marblefruit Prickly Pear (pg. 275)

Border Prickly Pear (pg. 279)

Chenille Prickly Pear (pg. 283)

Blind Prickly Pear (pg. 287)

Spinyfruit Prickly Pear (pg. 291)

Coastal Prickly Pear (pg. 295)

Englemann Prickly Pear (pg. 299)

Chisos Mountain Prickly Pear (pg. 303)

Common Dog Cholla (pg. 307)

Clumped Dog Cholla (pg. 311)

Big Bend Dog Cholla (pg. 315)

Icicle Cholla (pg. 319)

Thistle Cholla (pg. 323)

Desert Christmas Cholla (pg. 327)

Tree Cholla (pg. 331)

Desert Night-blooming Cactus (pg. 335)

Barbed Wire Cactus (pg. 339)

Check List/Index

Use the boxes to check cacti you've seen.

Photo Credits

All photos are copyright of their respective photographers as of 2009.

Steven J. Baskauf: 258 (spines), 297 (spines)

Chris Best/US Fish and Wildlife Service: 182 (flower), 184

Rick and Nora Bowers: 22 (both), 24, 25 (all), 26 (main, left), 28, 29 (all), 30 (all), 32, 33 (all), 34 (all), 36 (both), 37 (all), 38 (main, spines, fruit), 40 (both), 41 (all), 42 (spines, fruit), 44, 45 (left, middle), 46 (spines, flower, fruit), 48, 49 (all), 50 (all), 52, 53 (all), 54 (main, spines, flower), 56, 57 (all), 58 (all), 60, 61 (all), 62 (all), 64, 65 (all), 66 (all), 68, 69 (left, right), 70 (spines), 72, 73 (all), 74 (spines, flower, fruit), 76, 77 (all), 78 (main, spines, flower), 80, 81 (all), 82 (all), 84, 85 (all), 89 (all), 90 (main, spines, flower), 92 (both), 93 (all), 94 (both), 96, 97 (all), 98 (main, spines, flower), 100, 101 (middle, right), 102 (main, spines, flower), 104, 105 (all), 106 (spines), 109 (all), 110 (all), 112 (both), 113 (all), 114 (all), 116, 117 (all), 118 (all), 120, 121 (all), 122 (main, spines), 124, 125 (all), 126 (main, spines), 128, 129 (middle, right), 130 (main, spines, flower), 132, 133 (all), 134 (all), 136 (all), 137 (all), 138 (all), 140 (all), 141 (all), 142 (main, spines, flower), 144, 145 (all), 146 (main, spines), 148, 149 (all), 150 (all), 152, 153 (all), 154 (all), 156, 157 (all), 158 (all), 160 (both), 161 (all), 162 (all), 164, 165 (all), 166 (all), 168, 169 (all), 170 (all), 172 (both), 173 (all), 174 (all), 176, 177 (all), 178 (all), 180, 181 (all), 185 (middle, right), 186 (main, spines, flower), 189 (all), 190 (main, spines, flower), 193 (all), 194 (spines, flower, fruit), 196, 197 (all), 198 (all), 200 (all), 201 (all), 202 (main, spines, flower), 204 (all), 205 (all), 206 (main, spines fruit), 209 (all), 210 (all), 212, 213 (all), 214 (all), 216 (all), 217 (all), 218 (all), 220, 221 (all), 222 (both), 224, 225 (all), 226 (main, spines, fruit), 229 (all), 230 (all), 232 (both), 233 (all), 234 (all), 236, 237 (all), 245 (middle, right), 246 (spines, fruit), 249 (middle, right), 250 (main, spines, fruit), 252 (both), 253 (all), 254 (all), 256, 257 (left, right), 258 (fruit), 260, 261 (all), 262 (all), 264, 265 (all), 266 (flower, fruit), 268, 269 (all), 270 (all), 272, 273 (all), 274 (all), 276, 277 (all), 278 (main, spines, fruit), 280, 281 (all) 282 (glochids, flower), 285 (all), 286 (all), 288 (both), 289 (all), 290 (main, spines, flower), 292 (both), 293 (all), 298 (all), 300 (all), 301 (all), 302 (main, spines fruit), 304, 305 (all), 306 (main, spines, fruit), 309 (all), 310 (main, spines), 312, 313 (all), 314 (all), 316, 317 (left, right), 318 (main, spines, fruit), 320, 321 (right), 322 (spines), 324, 325 (all), 326 (all), 329 (all), 330 (all), 332 (main), 333 (left, middle), 334 (all), 336 (main), 337 (left, middle), 338 (main, spines), 340, 341 (all)

John Bregar: 86 (all), 88, 208, 308, 332 (skeleton)

James Cheshire: 238 (spines), 241 (left)

Will Cook: 240, 297 (right)

Shirley Denton: 294 (flower), 338 (fruit)

Erik F. Enderson: 134 (fruit)

Alan English: 328

Wally Gobetz: 294 (main, spines), 297 (left)

Alan Hahn: 69 (middle), 126 (flower), 129 (left)

Mary Ellen Harte: 245 (left)

Bill Hendricks/The Amateurs' Digest: 321 (middle), 322 (flower), 333 (right)

High Country Gardens: 186 (fruit)

Matthew B. Johnson: 26 (flower), 134 (main), 188 (main), 244 (both), 248

Eric Kiefer: 242 (fruit)

Gertrud Konings: 38 (flower), 42 (main), 45 (right), 54 (fruit), 70 (main), 74 (main), 78 (fruit), 98 (fruit), 101 (left), 102 (fruit), 106 (main, fruit), 108, 122 (fruit), 126 (fruit), 130 (fruit), 142 (fruit), 146 (flower, fruit), 182 (main, spines), 185 (left), 190 (fruit), 192, 194 (main), 198 (fruit), 202 (fruit), 206 (flower), 226 (flower), 228, 246 (main), 249 (left), 250 (flower), 257 (middle), 290 (fruit), 310 (fruit), 318 (flower), 321 (left), 322 (main, fruit), 337 (right), 338 (flower)

Jerry Murray: 241 (right), 242 (flower), 258 (main)

Gary D. Regner: 302 (flower)

S. Rutman: 336 (tuber)

Phillip Ruttenbur: 282 (main, fruit), 284, 306 (flower), 317 (middle)

Al Schneider: 242 (spines)

Joseph T. Smith II: 238 (fruit)

Stan Tekiela: 266 (main, spines)

Bob Upcavage: 294 (fruit), 296

Dorde Woodruff: 241 (middle), 242 (main)

www.southeasternflora.com: 238 (main)

About the Authors

Nora Mays Bowers

Nora Mays Bowers is a writer and nature photographer. She earned a Master of Science degree in Ecology from the University of Arizona, writing her thesis and publishing several professional papers on Harris's Hawks. Nora received grants from the National Science Foundation, Sigma Xi, Arizona Wildlife Foundation and James R. Silliman Memorial Research Fund for her hawk research, as well as research awards from the American Ornithologists' Union and Western Bird Banding Association. A member of the North American Nature Photography Association and Canon Professional Services, Nora's photography credits include *Birder's World Magazine*, *Ranger Rick* and *Arizona Wildlife Views*, as well as images in many books and calendars. She is coauthor of field guides for several other states, including *Wildflowers of Texas Field Guide*, *Wildflowers of Arizona Field Guide* and *Cactus of Arizona Field Guide*. She also coauthored *Kaufman Focus Guides: Mammals of North America*.

Rick Bowers

Rick Bowers is a nature photographer, naturalist and writer. He has been photographing wildlife and nature for more than 35 years. He received a Bachelor of Science degree in Wildlife Ecology from the University of Arizona. Before turning to professional photography and writing, he led nature tours for Victor Emanuel Nature Tours and his own tour company for 24 years. Rick led tours throughout the New World from Barrow, Alaska (the northernmost city in North America) to Tierra del Fuego (an island at